Easy Things to Make... To Make Things Easy

Easy Things To Make...
...To Make Things Easy

Simple Do-It-Yourself Home Modifications for Older People and Others with Physical Limitations

DOREEN BRENNER GREENSTEIN, Ph.D.
Cornell University

Illustrated by
SUZANNE BLOOM, B.F.A.

BROOKLINE BOOKS

ISBN 1-57129-024-9

Technical reviewers:

Mary Yearns, Ph.D.
*Department of Human Development and Family Studies,
Iowa State University*

Catherine Gordon, Ph.D., O.T.R.
Director, Occupational Therapy Department, Ithaca College

Jane Gay

Interior design and typography: Erica Schultz.

Library of Congress Cataloging-In-Publication Data
Greenstein, Doreen.
        Easy things to make-- to make things easy : simple do-it-yourself
    home modifications for older people and others with physical limitations /
    Doreen Brenner Greenstein : illustrated by Suzanne Bloom.
            p.   cm.
        Includes bibliographical references (p.   ).
        ISBN 1-57129-024-9 (pbk.)
        1. Self-help devices for the disabled. 2. Household applicances.
    3. Handicrafts. 4. Dwellings--Access for the physically
    handicapped. 5. Aged--Safety measures.   I. Title.
    HV1569.5.G74 1996
    362.4'048--dc20   96-24406
                                                                CIP

Published by
BROOKLINE BOOKS
P.O. Box 1047 • Cambridge, Massachusetts 02238
Order toll-free within the U.S.: 1-800-666-BOOK

I would like to especially thank Naomi Miner, O.T.R., who began this project with me, and Suzanne Bloom, the artist, who was very patient.

***

This book is dedicated to my parents, Michael and Paula Brenner, who appear on the front cover. With support from caring people, they were able to live independently, with pride, almost 'til the end.

C O N T E N T S

PREFACE

I'm sitting writing this in my old rural two-story house that my husband and I bought thirty years ago when our first child was a toddler. At that time, our thoughts were to buy a home for ourselves and our planned-for children. We still have our official measuring wall charting the growth of each of our children. Our kitchen cabinet still has the dent from its collision with my daughter's tricycle fender.

Our children are grown now; they've fledged—flown from our nest. But here we remain, my husband and I, in our cherished house that's too big, with a long driveway to shovel and a huge lawn to mow, with ten steps up to our bedroom and ten steps down to our basement, narrow doorways, old-fashioned bathrooms, and generally impossible conditions for anybody who might need to use a wheelchair or walker.

This book was written because as we age, many of us find ourselves living in environments that are not friendly to older people. Research has shown that elderly people who are most content with their housing situations are those who made a move early on, when their children were grown but when they were still relatively young (what do we call it now—late middle age? early retirement age?).

So moving into a low-maintenance, wheelchair-accessible dwelling makes sense. But I suspect my husband and I are not going to be among those sensible people, and neither are many of our friends and neighbors. So this book is written for my future self, for all the older people who need some hints to help make their living environment more accessible, and for their adult sons or daughters who can help make the changes. It's for friendly neighbors who are handy with a hammer, saw, sewing machine, or just tinkering. It's for care providers—public health nurses and personal attendants who help older people live as independently as possible.

The ideas in this book are not new. Many of them have been around for years, each solution thought of by an anonymous person who was good at solving problems. The book is not intended as a comprehensive answer to everybody's needs, nor are the suggestions offered perfect solutions, by any means. Rather, the purpose is to get you thinking about your own situation and get your creative ideas going. Give yourself a chance—you will find that you are your own best problem solver. If you have come up with a solution that you think would be helpful to others, please tell me about it. My address is:

330 Riley Robb Hall
Cornell University
Ithaca, NY 14853

Safety should be part of everything we do. There are safety messages scattered throughout this book. Please pay attention to them. Remember, though, that this safety information is not intended as a substitute for personal supervision. Although to the best of our ability, we have had the information and recommendations contained in this publication reviewed by experts, we make no guarantee as to—and assume no responsibility for—the correctness, sufficiency, or effectiveness of any of these modifications in solving a particular problem.

INTRODUCTION

Easy Things to Make... To Make Things Easy has been written to bring useful, easy-to-understand information to the whole family.

- The book includes low-cost special equipment (homemade and purchased) and home modifications. It speaks directly to the older readers who will be using the information in their own homes.

- The book also touches on caregivers' roles and concerns, with suggestions in each chapter to help caregivers balance their love, respect, and concern for the older person in their care.

- And finally, the book brings children into the picture as well, with many woodworking and sewing projects simple enough to be made by children as gifts for the older people in their lives.

In 1982, the National Long-Term Care Survey interviewed 6,000 older Americans with disabilities receiving Medicare benefits and living in the community. People were categorized as "disabled" if they reported being unable to eat, use the toilet, dress, get in or out of bed, or get to the bathroom without special equipment or help from another person.

The types of special equipment in the study included wheelchairs, railings, walkers, canes, crutches, bed lifts, raised toilet seats, adult briefs, bedpans, and catheters.

The same people were re-interviewed in 1984 and 1989 in order to track trends in the three main ways that people cope with chronic disability: help from another person; help from special equipment or housing modification; and a combination of special equipment and personal assistance. Between 1982 and 1989, the study found that:

- People were relying more on special equipment and housing modifications and less on personal assistance.

- Many people used a combination of special equipment and help from another person.

- A significantly greater proportion of respondents with disabilities reported using special equipment or housing modifications in 1989, compared with responses in 1982.[*]

[*] Manton, K., Corder, L., & Stallard, E. (1993). "Changes in the use of personal assistance and special equipment from 1982 to 1989: Results from the 1982 and 1989 NLTCS." *The Gerontologist*, vol. 33, no.2, pp. 168-176.

The results of the study are encouraging. For older people living with disabilities, use of special equipment, devices, or housing modifications may lessen the impact of the disabilities on their day-to-day enjoyment of life.

As a social policy, helping older people with disabilities remain at home with the help of special equipment or modifications may reduce the projected need for more nursing home beds in response to an aging population. We speak of "aging in place," an emotionless phrase that does not begin to describe people's powerful desire to stay in their own homes as they age. Without question, the most important part of a person's ability to stay in his home is the other people in his life — whether family members or paid assistants. However, it is reassuring that use of special equipment and home modifications is increasingly playing a positive role in older people's abilities to maintain their independence, in their own homes and in their own community.

Note: Some of the information in this introduction was taken from a report by the National Resource and Policy Center on Rural Long-Term Care, University of Kansas, August 1994.

CHAPTER 1

Bathroom & Washing Up

SINK MODIFICATIONS

Installing a Formica countertop with a new sink and lever-handled faucets may be the best way to make your sink accessible, but it is not always possible. There are other ways of making your bathroom sink more convenient for you.

- Make sure that any sink is strongly supported by brackets or legs. Support brackets can go back to the wall and don't have to take up floor space. Insulate exposed drain and hot-water pipes, especially if your legs are not temperature sensitive.

- A shelf that's next to the sink and within your reach can be very useful. Put a lip on the shelf so things don't roll off. Use brackets and supports to attach the shelf securely to the wall. Keep small items in a nonslip tray, which you can make or buy. Keep the tray on the sink counter or a convenient shelf. The tray should have edges to prevent small items from falling off.

- If you have enough floor space in your bathroom, a small cart with wheels can be a convenient and inexpensive alternative to a shelf.

• If you'll be seated while using the sink, you'll probably find that the medicine cabinet mirror is too high. Install an inexpensive, lightweight mirror at the proper height for you and make sure it's securely attached to the wall.

• If your faucet handles are difficult to turn, try installing new washers. Remove round faucet handles and buy cross-shaped, or "four-pointed cross," handles that will be easier for you to turn using your fist or wrist.

• You can construct lever handles for round faucet handles, using pipe-hanger brackets and radiator-hose clamps, as we show for the homemade lever door handle (p. 72). Or you can purchase commercially available faucet grippers from one of the specialty catalogs listed in the Resources section.

• Make sure the countertop is the right height for you. It should be high enough to fit your wheelchair under, and to provide some support if you stand up and lean on it. On the front edge or top surface of a countertop sink, install small grab bars or "D-shaped" door handles to hold on to.

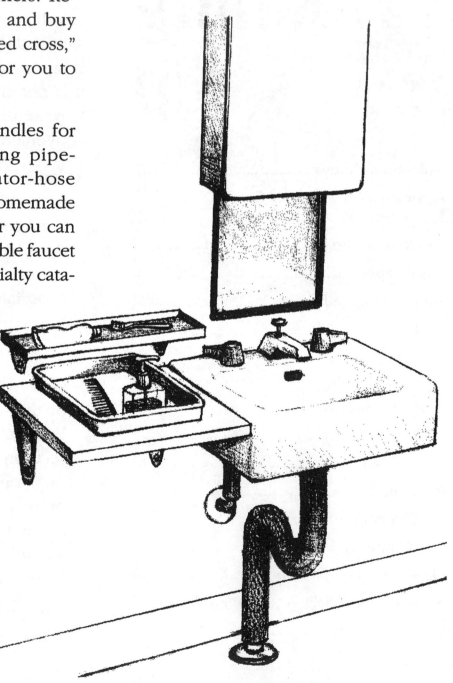

ADAPTING A CONVENTIONAL DROP-IN LAVATORY FOR WHEELCHAIR ACCESS

Replacing the bathroom sink is often the first change to be made to accommodate a person using a wheelchair. Although many "special" wall-hung sinks on the market are designed to meet federal standards, they are often expensive, require nonstandard construction, and can be institutional in appearance.

With minor modification of conventional cabinet construction, a conventional lavatory sink can be installed to provide knee space that meets most standards. The Center for Accessible Housing at North Carolina State University has developed guide-

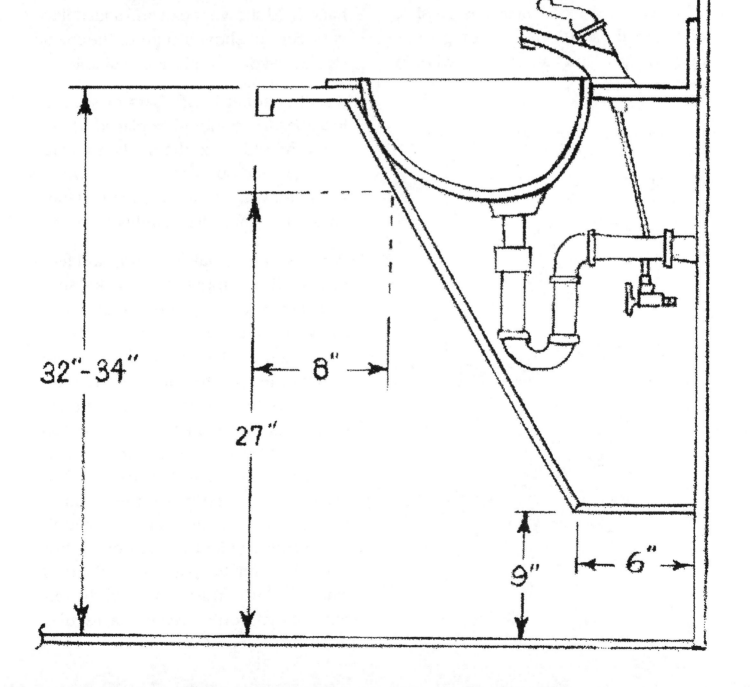

lines for installing a typical drop-in lavatory in a way that is wheelchair-accessible and meets federal standards.

The conventional drop-in lavatory shown here provides knee space that exceeds federal standards. The counter height may need to be raised 1" to 2" above standard vanity height (32"), allowing the underside of the 7" to 8" sink to clear the 27" minimum knee space requirement. Select as shallow a sink as possible, and make sure the drain is toward the back of the bowl so you have as much knee space as possible.

If these illustrations do not provide enough details, you can obtain further information from:

Center for Accessible Housing
School of Design
North Carolina State University
Box 8613
Raleigh, NC 27695-8613

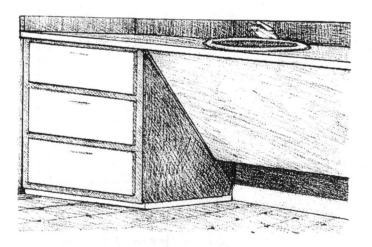

TUB MODIFICATIONS

If you are building a house or redoing your bathroom, you can install a walk-in shower enclosure that is designed for people who have difficulty getting in and out of a bathtub. However, if you have a traditionally styled tub and shower, and you want to modify it without spending a lot of money, the following ideas may be helpful.

- Purchase a commercially available hand-held shower head and attach it to your current shower fixture. Inexpensive do-it-yourself kits are available.

- Install adequate grab bars in several locations. They should be placed where you can hold on to them when you're getting in and out of the tub, and when you're moving around in the tub. Grab bars must be installed safely (see p. 8).

- Purchase a tub chair with nonskid feet at a medical supply store. Make sure you choose a sturdy one. The sturdiest shower chair is really a bench, with four legs inside the bathtub and two more legs that rest on the floor outside the tub. Unlike ordinary chairs, commercially made tub chairs are designed to be the right size and shape for use in a bathtub. These special chairs are often available (on loan or for free) from a local agency such as your Cancer Society or Independent Living Center. But a tub chair that fits your tub well and is sturdy and waterproof is worth the extra money. Don't *ever* use a regular chair as a tub chair.

(Unfortunately, a few people insist on using a regular chair in the tub, so this comment is for them: Make sure that you use a sturdy, non-folding chair that fits well in your tub and has nonslip feet on it, such as crutch tips. But the only really good idea is to use a commercial tub chair.)

• For safety, it's important that the shower enclosure be well lit. Use a transparent shower curtain—it allows more light in.

• If the water in your shower gets hot when someone flushes the toilet or turns on the cold water, install an anti-scald device on the shower head. These are easy-to-install, commercially available devices that shut the water off automatically if it gets too hot (see p. 38).

• There may sometimes be a problem with water spraying out of the tub when you are using a hand-held shower head or when you are sitting on a wide tub chair. Try using one and a half or two shower curtains, instead of one, so that there is extra curtain material. In this way, you can draw the two curtains together at the center of the tub and overlap them, rather than leaving a gap at the front or the back of the enclosure. A couple of spring-type clothespins can be used to fasten the two curtains together while you shower. To prevent falls, keep a mop handy to clean up any water that has dripped onto the floor.

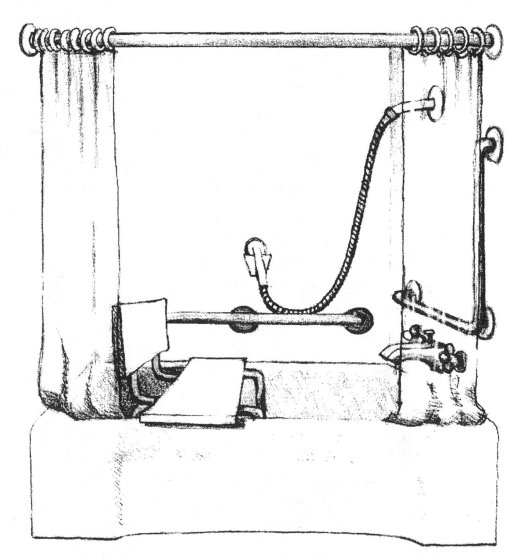

TOILET PAPER

Many people, especially if they only have the use of one hand, complain that when they try to use the toilet paper it unrolls too quickly. They tell us that it's difficult to tear off a piece of toilet paper without the whole roll spinning out of control. Here are some simple solutions to this problem:

- Before you put a new roll of toilet paper on the roller, squash the roll so the hole in the cardboard cylinder is oval instead of round. The toilet paper won't unroll as quickly.

- Some toilet-paper holders can be removed from the wall, turned 90 degrees, and re-installed so the roll is held in a vertical position. The roll's weight on the holder makes it less likely to unroll too quickly.

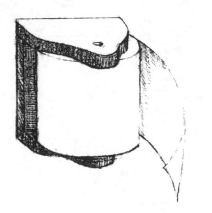

- Attach the short edge of a scrap of terry cloth or corduroy fabric (about 3" x 5") to the toilet-paper roller with tape as shown. Snugly wrap the fabric around the roller and tape or glue the loose end in place. The friction between the roll's paper cylinder and the fabric on the roller makes the toilet paper unroll more slowly.

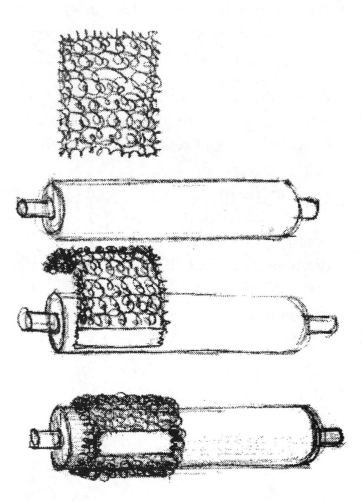

Another big problem is trying to insert a new roll of toilet paper. There is a new style of toilet-paper dispenser that has two "flippers" instead of a roller; this enables you to replace the roll with one hand. These dispensers can be found in most home-supply stores.

SAFETY IN THE BATHROOM

Because the bathroom is the most dangerous room in a house, it's well worth taking time to review some safety precautions.

- A nonslip floor surface is essential in the bathtub or shower. A single, small rubber bath mat in the tub is not enough, nor are stick-on appliqués, because they leave too much slippery tub bottom exposed. Use a rubber bath mat that covers the entire bottom of the tub. If you can't find a single large bath mat, use two or three smaller ones to cover the tub bottom.

- Don't add bath oil to your bath water. It can make the tub very slippery.

- Wet floors can be dangerous. Keep your bathroom floor dry.

- A nonskid floor covering or a rubber-backed bath rug next to the tub is essential. The rubber backing will last longer if you don't dry the rug in your dryer.

- Grab bars should be installed in several locations in the bathroom, wherever you need them to help you steady yourself.

- If you're unsteady on your feet, place a sturdy chair in the bathroom so you can sit down when you need to rest. Place a convenient grab bar near the chair to hold onto when you're getting up or sitting down.

- Space heaters are particularly dangerous. You can fall against a hot heater, and if you have reduced feeling in your legs, you can burn yourself without realizing it. Even if a heater isn't turned on, you can trip over it or hurt yourself on its sharp edges. Consider a safer alternative, such as a heat lamp installed in the ceiling.

- For your safety and convenience, make sure the lighting is adequate. "Night lighting" is very important in the bathroom. Install an automatic night-light that turns itself on and off. Use an illuminated or glow-in-the-dark light switch.

- Install ground-fault-interrupted (GFI) outlets in the bathroom. These outlets prevent deadly electrical shocks. Most newer homes have GFI outlets as required by the building code. If your older home lacks them, it is highly recommended that you have them installed.

GRAB BARS

Grab bars can be helpful when you need to change position (such as getting on or off the toilet), or when you want to steady yourself in a slippery place (like the bathtub or shower). They are sold in plumbing and home building supply stores. Towel racks or protruding soap dishes should never be used as grab bars. And grab bars should never be used as towel racks—they must remain uncovered at all times so they can be grabbed.

Essential features to check for when selecting and installing grab bars include:

- "fit" for your hand and safety clearance from the mounting surface

- materials, shapes, and grip-surface treatment

- placement and ability to support your weight

Fit and clearance: Most people prefer a round or oval shape 1½" in diameter. If the grab bar is oval, the long dimension should be parallel to the wall. Clearance should allow comfortable reaching and gripping, but

prevent your arm from sliding down between the grab bar and the wall—1½" from the wall is generally enough.

Materials: Grab bars with a textured grip surface (like the one shown here) should be installed in areas where your hands will be wet or soapy—in the tub or near a sink, for example. There are many different shapes and sizes to choose from. Think about your bathroom and how you will use the grab bar.

Placement: Where you place a grab bar depends on whether you will lean, push, or pull on it; whether you have a "strong" and "weak" side; what range of reach is comfortable; and whether you use a wheelchair. You can place a grab bar horizontally, vertically, or at an angle. There are straight grab bars (like the one shown here) and L-shaped grab bars.

Ability to support your weight: The grab bar must be able to support at least 250 pounds, and must be screwed into the wall studs. You may need to remove wall covering and sheetrock to insert backing and anchoring boards between studs (generally 2" x 8" or 2" x 10" boards nailed between the studs). If you have tile or plaster walls, you cannot use molly bolts; installation of grab bars may require professional help.

Note: The information on this page is taken, in part, from a fact sheet published by the Minnesota Housing Finance Agency, 400 Sibley St., Suite 33, St. Paul, MN 55101.

BUILT-UP HANDLES FOR HAIRBRUSH AND TOOTHBRUSH

Hairbrush

If you have difficulty grasping things, or if you prefer having a handle that is soft to hold, you can build up the handle of your hairbrush.

Use hot-water-pipe insulation made of preshaped foam and wrap it with plastic tape. Tape comes in many colors, so you can choose one that matches your decor.

1. Take a short piece of hot-water-pipe insulation (available at hardware and plumbing stores), and cut a section the length of your hairbrush handle.

2. Use pipe insulation with an inner diameter that will fit snugly around your hairbrush handle. If this makes it too bulky, you can cut a lengthwise wedge out of the insulation to make it fit better (see p. 44 for detailed instructions).

3. Fit the insulation snugly around the hairbrush handle and wrap it tightly with plastic tape, as shown.

Toothbrush

You can also create a simple, built-up handle for your toothbrush, but you will want to make it out of something washable.

1. Take a piece of terry cloth or an old washcloth.

2. Fold the washcloth into a rectangle whose short side is a little shorter than the handle.

3. Wrap it snugly around the toothbrush handle as shown in the picture.

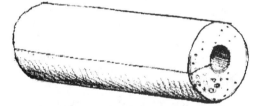

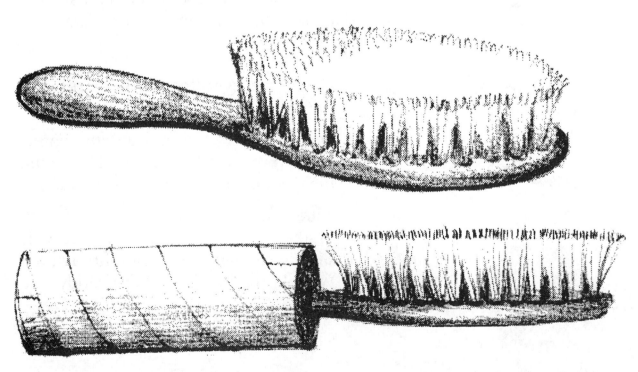

4. Fasten it with a couple of rubber bands or ponytail holders.

It's easy to take the toothbrush grip off when you want to launder the cloth.

If it is hard for you to manipulate a regular toothbrush, try an electric one. For cleaning dentures, a nail brush or vegetable brush works well and will be easier to hold onto than a toothbrush.

LIQUID-SOAP CADDY

Try this caddy if you prefer to use liquid soap but find the dispenser is slippery or hard to hold. The caddy has a nonslip bottom, and its weight keeps it stable when you pump the soap. This caddy design fits most liquid-soap containers. If your container has nonstandard dimensions, adjust the pattern accordingly.

You will need:

1 piece of 1" x 3" lumber (finished size ¾" x 2½") 3" long (base)
2 pieces of 1" x 3" lumber (finished size ¾" x 2½") 4½" long (sides)
2 ¼" dowels 5" long
2 ¼" dowels 4½" long
4 ornamental knobs or beads with ¼" hole (from a craft store)
4 brads 1¼" long
sandpaper
glue
waterproof paint or polyurethane
paint, stencils, or other decorations
silicone bathroom tub and tile sealant

Directions:

1. Cut all pieces to the correct sizes. Cut the two sides as shown in the picture.

2. Drill two sets of ¼" holes with centers ¼" in from the edges, 2" and 3" up from the bottom, as shown in the picture.

3. Glue a knob on one end only of each of the 5" dowels. Sand the dowels slightly so they can be slid through the ¼" holes in the sides of the caddy.

4. Glue and nail the base and sides of the caddy together.

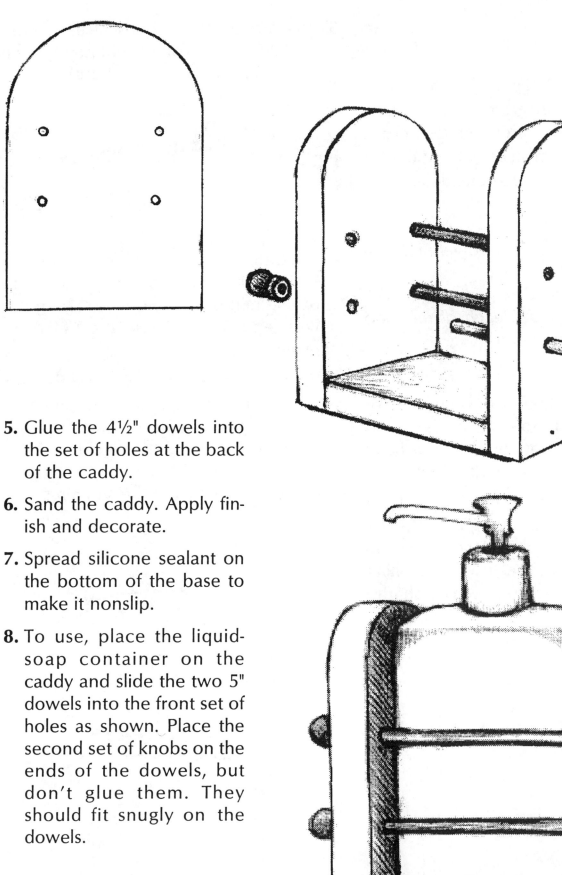

5. Glue the 4½" dowels into the set of holes at the back of the caddy.

6. Sand the caddy. Apply finish and decorate.

7. Spread silicone sealant on the bottom of the base to make it nonslip.

8. To use, place the liquid-soap container on the caddy and slide the two 5" dowels into the front set of holes as shown. Place the second set of knobs on the ends of the dowels, but don't glue them. They should fit snugly on the dowels.

BATH MITT

This soap mitt can keep a bar of soap from slipping out of your grasp. Accompanied by fragrant soap or after-bath powder, a soap mitt made from a pretty hand or dish towel can be a special handmade gift.

You will need:

1 terry-cloth hand or dish towel (approximately 14 x 24")

1 two-part 3" piece of ½" wide sew-on Velcro fastener tape (3" each of the loop part and the hook part)

Directions:

1. Trace the solid line of this mitt pattern on paper. This is your *sewing* line. Add ½" all the way around (1" if your hand is very large) for your *cutting* line.

2. Fold the towel in half, matching hemmed ends. Cut along the fold line so you have two equal pieces. Place the paper pattern on the towel, matching the wrist end of pattern with the hemmed ends. Cut around the pattern. You now have two mitt pieces.

3. Overlap by ½" the ends of the pieces of Velcro tape. You should now have a 5½" long strip (as shown here).

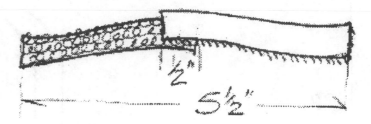

4. Separate the two mitt pieces. Lay the Velcro strip on the right (decorated) side of one mitt piece, about 1½" from the wrist end. Baste or pin the Velcro in place.

5. With right sides together, stitch the two mitt pieces together along the stitching line, sewing through the basted-in Velcro tape. Reinforce the stitching at the wrist ends. Clip the seam at the base of the thumb, almost to the stitching.

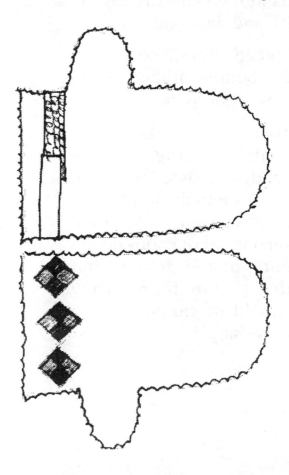

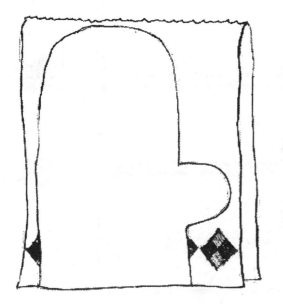

6. To prevent the rough end of the Velcro strip from rubbing your wrist, cut it off close to the seam. Turn the mitt right side out.

7. To use the mitt, put it on your hand and slip a small bar of soap inside the palm. Fasten the Velcro strap snugly. Wet the mitt and work up a lather.

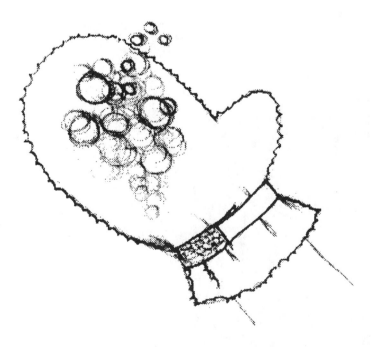

GETTING YOURSELF DRY

Here are some hints about drying yourself after washing.

- A terry-cloth bathrobe can be a substitute for a bath towel. Wrapping up in the robe will get you dry and keep you warm as well. Remember, if one arm is weaker than the other, first put your weaker arm all the way into the robe's sleeve by guiding it in with your stronger arm. Then put your stronger arm in its sleeve.

- If drying is difficult, or if you have difficulty holding a bath towel, cut a wide strip of toweling and sew large cloth or webbing loop handles on both ends of the strip. You can slip your hands through the handles to dry your back and other hard-to-reach areas.

- If bathing takes a long time, it can be a chilling experience. To avoid such chills, sew a simple terry-cloth jacket, or cut off the bottom half of an old terry-cloth robe. To stay warm, cover the bottom half of your body with a large bath towel and wash your top half first. Then you can wrap yourself in your terry-cloth bath jacket while you wash your bottom half.

- To dry between your toes if you can't bend, cover the end of a yardstick with a snug-fitting terry-cloth "slipcover" and reach between your toes with it.

NAIL CLIPPER

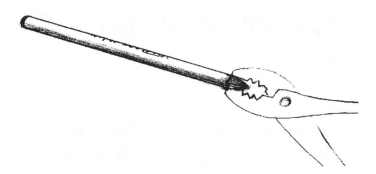

Try this stabilized nail clipper. The long handle provides extra leverage so it's easier to use. The nonslip base keeps the nail clipper steady.

You will need:

1 regular nail clipper
1 5" long piece of 1" x 3" lumber (finished size ¾" x 2½") or other similar piece of scrap lumber
1 # 6 x ¾" roundheaded screw
1 discarded stick-type ballpoint pen
silicone bathtub and tile sealant
sandpaper
paint or polyurethane finish if desired

Directions:

1. Cut your piece of lumber to size, sand it, and apply finish if desired.

2. Center the nail clipper on one end of the piece of lumber, allowing it to stick out ½".

3. Use a pencil to mark the position under the hole in the nail clipper.

4. On the mark, drill a small pilot hole in the wood.

5. Put a dab of sealant on the underside of the nail clipper. Attach the nail clipper to the wood block with the screw.

6. Take the pen apart as shown in the picture. Use a pair of pliers to extract the ink cartridge if you can't twist the pen apart with your hands.

7. Slip the empty pen shaft over the handle of the nail clipper. Force the shaft all the way to the base of the handle, or as far as you can push it on.

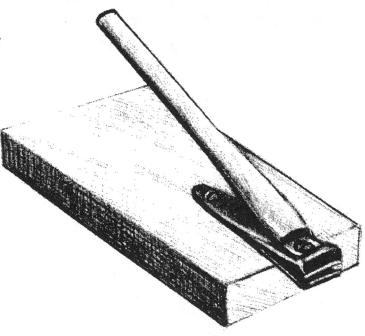

8. To create a nonslip surface, spread a thin coating of silicone bathtub and tile sealant on the underside of the wood block, or glue a piece of nonslip mesh rug backing to the underside.

HAVE YOU THOUGHT ABOUT THIS?

- Bathrooms never seem to have enough counter storage space. One key to managing in the bathroom is organization. Small, inexpensive rollaway carts are available at most discount stores. Remember, though, that these carts are not strong or stable enough to help you support yourself.

- Keep your supplies handy. To minimize clutter, get rid of things you don't use, or store them away. Keep an extra set of cleaning supplies tucked into a corner.

- If you don't see too well, use brightly colored towels and washcloths. They're easier to see against light-colored bathroom walls.

- Use a ceiling-mounted heat lamp to warm the room before your bath or shower. That way, you don't have to turn on your whole heating system and you don't have to use a space heater. Just turn on the heat lamp for a few moments when you first come into the bathroom, and for a few moments after you get out of the shower or tub.

- Use nonslip trays and compartmentalized containers to help you keep things within reach.

- For safety's sake, go through your medicine cabinet and throw away old, outdated prescriptions. Keep medications in their properly labeled and dated containers.

- Install a telephone in your bathroom. In an emergency you'll have a phone right there, and if the phone rings while you're in the bathroom, you can easily get the call. If you get a small "wall" phone, you can mount it inside the door of your lavatory vanity. The phone will be out of sight and if you fall, you can still get to it to call for help. Or, if you use a wheelchair, you can carry a small cordless phone in a bag attached to your wheelchair.

- Install an inexpensive anti-scald device such as the Scald-Safe Faucet Hot-Water Sensor (Resources Conservation Company, of Greenwich, Connecticut) that screws onto a sink faucet or shower head. It shuts off the flow if the water gets too hot.

- If possible, your bathroom door should open outward. That way a fallen person cannot block the bathroom door and prevent it from opening when help arrives. Make sure that the door lock can be opened from both sides.

SOME COMMERCIALLY AVAILABLE PRODUCTS

Many handy devices for helping in the bathroom are available from medical supply stores or through specialty catalogs:

- **Raised toilet seats** can be secured to a standard toilet bowl, raising the seat height to 18". It is easier for you to sit down and stand up when you are sitting on a higher seat. Many styles are available. Some people find that a removable plastic raised toilet seat works best because it is easy to clean, and it can be removed so it doesn't interfere with other family members' use of the bathroom.

  If you are traveling, or if you can't install a permanent raised toilet seat and grab bars, you can use a commode chair (with the pail removed) on top of the toilet. However, this arrangement will not be as stable as regular grab bars, so it may not work for you if you need a lot of support.

- **Suction-cup brushes** attach to your sink or countertop with large suction cups. You can then scrub your nails and hand without needing to hold the brush in your other hand. A suction-cup denture brush can be attached with two suction cups to a wall, countertop, or sink so you can clean your dentures with one hand. You can also use Velcro to attach a brush to your sink, countertop, or wall.

- **Toothpaste tube squeezers** can be used with most tubes (toothpaste, hand cream, etc.) They are easy to use and sit on a sturdy base.

- **Long-handled bath brushes or sponges** can be used to clean you or the tub. Many styles are available.

- **Dental floss holders** let you floss your teeth with one hand. Several different designs are available.

- **Toilet flush-lever extensions** fit most toilets. They allow you to flush easily using your hand, elbow, or forearm.

- **Small urinals** are available for women as well as for men. These can be used either standing or sitting.

- **Toilet paper tongs** can be useful if your reach is limited. The tongs hold the toilet tissue securely in place and allow you to care for your intimate hygiene needs.

CAREGIVER NOTES

It can be hard for an older person to have to ask for help with everyday bathroom tasks. It can be hard for us, as caregivers, to create a balance between encouraging independence, worrying about safety, and accomplishing what needs to get done.

These are not easy concerns to balance, and our choices are made more difficult because privacy in the bathroom is so highly valued in our culture, and because bathroom designers seem so determined to make things difficult to modify.

So how do we balance our concerns with an older person's wishes to be self-sufficient?

- Survey the bathroom. Make sure that everything is as safe as possible. Think of what you need for the present, but also plan for the future.

- Look at accessibility. Think of changes that will make bathroom activities as comfortable as possible.

- Get the bathroom user involved at the planning stage. Radical changes may never be especially welcome, but planning bathroom modifications together can help make those changes more acceptable.

- Get professional advice. If you are helping plan for a patient being discharged from a hospital, involve a physical and/or occupational therapist in decisions about bathroom modifications as well as in helping to adapt specific bathroom tasks and activities.

- Reassurance is important. While the changes may seem strange or different now, once new ways of doing things are learned, getting along in the bathroom will be a lot safer and more comfortable.

- If extensive modifications are planned, consult specialists, and refer to the accessibility and design books listed in the resource chapter. There are specific guidelines for modifying bathrooms to accommodate people with disabilities.

CHAPTER

Bedroom  & Getting Dressed

BED ADJUSTMENTS

What height is best for your bed? You may not even be aware of it, but the height of your bed may be making it difficult for you to get in or out of bed. You may want your bed at the same height as your wheelchair seat (typically 18" to 19" high) so you can transfer back and forth between your bed and your chair more easily. You may want your bed higher than it is now so you can stand up more easily when you're sitting on the edge of the bed. Or, you may want your bed lower because your feet don't reach the floor when you're sitting on the edge of the bed.

Whatever changes you want to make, safety is a primary concern. It is easy to fall out of bed, especially when you're just waking up. You must make sure that your bed is stable after you have adjusted the height. Your bed must never be able to slip off the supports you've put under it.

Not all beds can be modified, but here are a few suggestions that may work for your bed. Of course, the style, material, and design of the bed legs will determine whether or not the bed height can be adjusted.

- Lowering your bed may be as simple as cutting off equal lengths from each bed leg or removing the casters. Put caps or glides on the bottom of each leg to protect your floor.

- Methods for raising the bed will depend on what type of legs your bed has. Tall boxes can be made for each leg, with space inside each box for a wooden insert to raise the bed height. Some bed legs can be drilled so that leg extensions can be bolted on securely. Be very careful to make the modifications safe. However you raise your bed, you want to be absolutely certain that the bed leg extender cannot collapse, break, or fall off.

- Even if the bed's height isn't a factor, having a bed on wheels can be a problem. Take the casters off, or lock them, so that the bed doesn't roll out from underneath you while you are getting in or out of it. If you take the casters off, put rubber or nylon caps on the bottoms of the bed legs to avoid scraping the floor.

KEEPING BLANKETS OFF YOUR FEET

Does the weight of bedding on your feet bother you? With PVC pipe, you can make a simple, inexpensive blanket support to solve the problem.

You will need:
1 10' piece of ½" PVC pipe
8 PVC elbow fittings
2 PVC tee fittings
PVC adhesive (use in a well-ventilated area)

Using a kitchen scrubber and dish detergent, scrub the black printing off the PVC pipe. Cut the pipe into two 5' lengths. Cut one 5' length into 6 pieces as illustrated below: 2, 8, 8, 10, 16, and 16 inches. Cut the other 5' length into 5 pieces: 2, 10, 16, 16, and 16 inches.

- **Making the top and bottom units (each finished unit resembles a "U"):**

1. Glue an elbow onto one end of each 8" piece and each 10" piece.

2. Glue the two 8" pieces to a 16" piece, forming a "U." Make sure the unit lies flat after the pieces are glued together. Do the same with the two 10" pieces and a 16" piece. The 8" "U" will be the

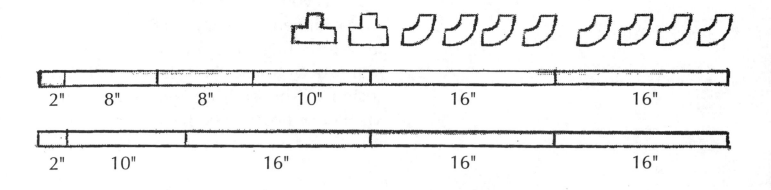

| 2" | 8" | 8" | 10" | 16" | 16" |

| 2" | 10" | 16" | 16" | 16" |

top of the blanket support; the 10" "U" will be the base.

3. Glue an elbow to the unattached end of each 8" piece and each 10" piece so that the opening of each elbow is perpendicular to the "U."

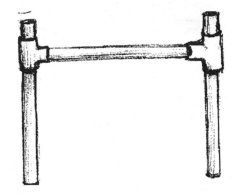

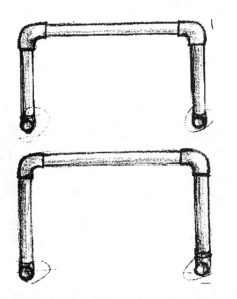

"U." Slip the 10" base between your mattress and box spring. Drape your blankets over the blanket support. The unit is very flexible and strong.

- **Making the vertical support unit (this finished unit resembles an "H"):**

4. Glue together a 2" piece and a 16" piece with a tee fitting. Do the same thing with the other 2" piece and a 16" piece. These form the two vertical sides.

5. Glue the two sides together with a 16" piece, forming an "H" with a short top part and a long bottom part, as shown in the illustration (above right). Make sure the unit lies flat after it's glued.

- **Assembling the blanket support:**

6. Glue the short ends of the "H" into the elbows on the 8" "U." Glue the long ends of the "H" into the elbows on the 10"

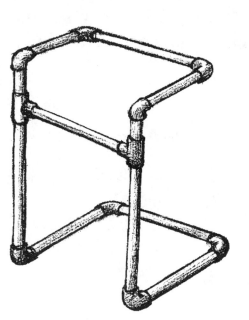

HOT PAD

A hot pad is very soothing for arthritis and other aches and pains. This convenient hot pad,* made from a dish or hand towel, drapes very comfortably over your knee, shoulder, or neck, or wherever else you need moist heat. Select a towel that has a design on it or is colored, since a white towel may become discolored with use. This is a simple sewing project and would make a nice gift for a grandparent. Caution must be taken when using the hot pad because it can get very hot, so be careful if the person using it is somewhat insensitive to heat.

You will need:

1   dish towel or hand towel, measuring approximately 15 x 24"
2   pounds of uncooked white rice (not "minute" rice)
2   tablespoons of dried lavender flowers or other potpourri (optional)

Directions:

1. Cut the towel in half, as shown. Each half will make one hot pad. Remove any fringe from the edges.

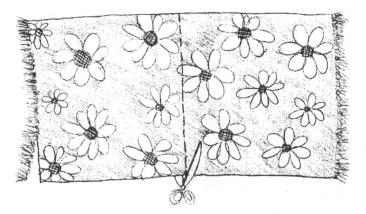

*Thanks to Jane Gay for this idea.

2. Fold one of the towel halves in half lengthwise, with the decorated side inside. Pin it and sew around the three open sides, leaving a 3" opening, as shown. Use small stitches so none of the rice will leak out.

3. Turn the towel right side out (so the design shows). Pour the raw white rice (along with the dried lavender or potpourri, if you want to use it) into the 3" opening.

4. Tuck in the seam allowance and sew the opening closed. Use an overcast stitch (as shown here) or sew it on a sewing machine.

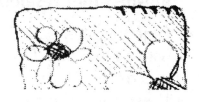

To use the hot pad, heat it in a microwave oven at full power for three to four minutes. You may need to adjust the time for your particular microwave oven.

The hot pad produces a lot of moist heat. If it proves to be too uncomfortable, put a cloth between your skin and the hot pad. You can regulate the heat of the hot pad by putting it in your microwave for a shorter or longer period of time.

CAUTION: *Never* put this heating pad on a person who cannot move away from the heat or a person who cannot feel heat.

DRESSERS AND KNOBS

Dresser drawers can be difficult to open; the drawers often have small knobs or fancy handles that are difficult to grasp. Luckily, dresser drawers can often be easily modified. We have shown different modifications on each of the four dresser drawers in the illustration.

- The small knobs on the top drawer of this dresser have been replaced with larger cabinet door knobs, available in many sizes and shapes at hardware stores or lumber yards. Square knobs may be easier to grasp than round ones.

- On the second drawer, the knobs have been replaced with inexpensive towel bars attached with screws to the drawers. Instead of having to use two knobs or handles, you can grasp the towel bar with one hand. Of course, this modification will create extra holes in the wood.

- The third drawer shows how you can make your own handle by drilling holes in dowels and in wooden spacers. Run bolts through the dowels and spacers, into the existing holes in the drawer. Make sure there is 1½" to 2" of clearance between the dowel and the drawer.

- As shown on the fourth drawer, you can replace the knobs with eye-bolts and tie a piece of soft rope between the bolts. (Or you can knot the ends of the rope around the existing handles on each drawer.) You can mark the center of the rope with colored tape to make it easier to see where to grasp it, or tie a knot in the center of the rope handle.

Make sure the drawers slide easily on their tracks. If they don't, try an old-fashioned remedy: waxing the drawer slides by rubbing them with a candle or a ball of kitchen wax paper. Also, make sure that your dresser drawers are not overloaded, so that they are light enough to open easily.

If your dresser is difficult to use, you may find that a dresser in another room is more suited to your current needs. Even if it's too small, you can keep things in it that you use frequently, and store other things elsewhere.

DRESSING TABLE

This idea may be for you if you sit down while you brush your hair or put on makeup, or if you need a central place to take care of all those other tasks that are done in front of a mirror. People generally keep things on top of their dressers, but many dresser tops are too high to reach comfortably, and dresser mirrors are too high to see yourself in if you're sitting down.

• One thing you can do is to set yourself up with a dressing table or vanity table. Any simple table will do, as long

as the height is good for you. If you use a wheelchair, make sure the table is high enough for you.

- Provide yourself with a sturdy chair for comfortable sitting. You may find that a swivel office chair (with or without arms) works well for you. You can paint your new vanity set, or put a skirt around the table.

- Hang a lightweight mirror above your new dressing table so that you can see yourself comfortably. An additional small table-top magnifying mirror will give you a close-up view.

- Add an adjustable table lamp for good lighting, but to avoid annoying glare, don't let the light reflect in the mirror.

- A lightweight, inexpensive rolling cart may be a useful place to store some supplies. You can tuck it under the dressing table or into a corner when it is not needed.

- To keep small items from slipping or rolling out of your reach, store them in trays or bins with edges, or place them on a soft, nonslip placemat.

- Make your hairbrush handle bigger and softer for easy gripping (see instructions on p. 9).

- Make "nests" out of scrap styrofoam pieces to stabilize small bottles or containers of liquid that tend to tip over.

CLOSET MODIFICATIONS

There are many types of closet modifications. Your choice of modifications will depend on your preferences and the layout of your house. The closet renovations don't have to be as pretty as a magazine photo to be useful. You can make some simple, inexpensive changes. Think about which of these suggestions will work best for you.

- Lower the closet rod to a height that is comfortable to reach.

- Put in a shelf above your lowered closet rod for extra storage room.

- Use extra-thick plastic hangers if you have a difficult time holding onto things.

- Store frequently worn garments on hooks.

- Build a shelf about 12" off the closet floor. You can store things on the shelf and not have to bend all the way down to the floor.

- We tend to hang onto clothes that we really don't use anymore. Donate some of your unneeded clothing to a church or charity. You'll have more space, and others will benefit from your generosity.

- Store infrequently used items in rectangular laundry baskets on the floor. Attach a good-sized loop of soft rope as a handle on the end of each basket (for pulling them out of the closet) if you can't grip things well.

- Take the door off the closet and replace it with a curtain. Use large, café-type curtain rings to make sure that the curtain is easy to slide.

- Install a lightweight bi-fold door with a big handle on it for easy gripping, or put in a sliding door (with a large handle) on a track.

ZIPPERS AND GARMENT FASTENINGS

If buttons pose a problem for you, try one of these ideas:

- Replace buttons with large snaps or hooks, if either of these devices is easier for you to fasten.

- Use Velcro instead of buttons.

- Extend the buttons on long-sleeved shirt cuffs with elastic, so that the cuff does not have to be buttoned or unbuttoned when you dress. Use an elastic ponytail holder (diameter approximately 1") and fasten it in the button hole as illustrated below.

- If you have problems with your vision, look for garments with stitching and buttons in a contrasting color.

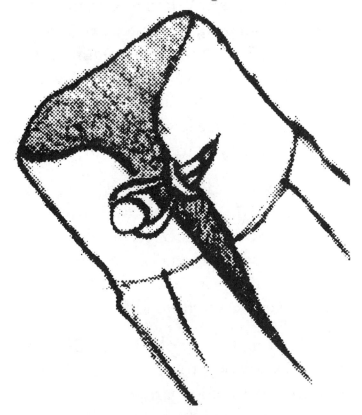

If you have a hard time grasping a zipper pull, try one of these solutions:

- Fasten a key ring or key chain to the existing zipper pull, or make a small ribbon loop in the zipper pull. For the zipper pull on your trousers, use a less visible loop of transparent nylon fishing line.

- Buy garments with large zipper pulls, or replace existing zippers with new ones that have larger zipper pulls.

- To use a jacket with a two-part zipper up the front, try purchasing a garment one size larger than usual, leaving the bottom closed (sew it together if you wish), and putting the jacket on as a pullover. A better solution for a jacket is to use Velcro strips instead of a zipper.

When you are buying clothes, look for:

- Pull-on pants with expandable, elastic waists.

- Garments with as few fasteners as possible.

- Loose, roomy styles with front openings.

- Moderately stretchy fabrics. (Clothing that is too stretchy may be a problem.)

Velcro to Fasten your Garments

Velcro fastener tape comes in many different colors and can be used to match the colors and styles of all kinds of clothing. For clothing modifications, choose Velcro that must be sewn on. Adhesive-backed Velcro does not hold up to the stress of repeated washing and the strain it gets as a fastener on clothing.

Each strip of Velcro has two parts: one part has a rough (hook) surface, and the matching part has a fuzzy (loop) surface. Make sure you sew the part with the rough surface so that it is facing away from your skin, to prevent it from rubbing against you. Also make sure that there are no sharp corners on the Velcro pieces to irritate your

skin. Here are some ideas to try.

- Take the buttons off a shirt. Sew short pieces of Velcro strip where the buttons were, and short pieces of matching Velcro underneath the buttonholes. Then you can fasten your shirt with a stroke of your hand. If you reattach the buttons right over the buttonholes, they give the appearance that your shirt is buttoned, while the Velcro is really holding the shirt closed.

- Use Velcro to make a neck hole larger, on a sweater for instance. Starting at the neck hole on one side, open the shoulder seam part way. Sew one part of a Velcro strip along the top edge and sew the matching part on the underside of the shoulder seam. This makes it easier to pull the sweater on over your head.

- If you have difficulty zipping your clothing, sew strips of Velcro next to the zipper on your skirt, pants, coat, or jacket. You may have to take the garment to someone who has an industrial sewing machine to modify a coat or jacket. A garment one size larger than usual may be easier for you to get on and off.

- Buy ready-made clothing with Velcro fasteners. J.C. Penney (see the Resources section) is one company that offers a special catalog of attractive easy-dressing clothes, many of which use Velcro as the fastener.

Velcro is rough, so close Velcro fasteners before laundering to prevent lint pickup and damage to other garments.

DRESSING STICK

Using a dressing stick can make dressing and undressing easier. Think of a dressing stick as an extension of your arm, and the hook on the end as your fingers. You can use the hook to pull or push with. For example, holding the dressing stick, you can slip its hook through your pants belt loop and pull up your pants. Or you can pull a sweater up over your shoulder.

You will need:

1 ⁵/₈" dowel about 24" long (or slightly longer or shorter, depending on your size)
1 plastic-covered wire coat and hat hook, available at hardware stores

Directions:

1. Drill a small pilot hole in one end of the dowel.

2. Wrap the hook in masking tape to protect the plastic finish.

3. Grip the hook with a pipe wrench or monkey wrench as shown. Bend the end of the hook with your hand or against a hard surface to form a right angle.

4. Unwrap and discard tape. Screw the hook into the pilot hole in the end of the dowel.

5. Sand the other end of the dowel so it doesn't catch on clothing.

Sew small loops of ribbon or seam binding inside your clothes (at the waistband for example) that you can catch with the hook of your dressing stick. Using a contrasting color will make the loops easier for you to see while you're getting dressed.

An emergency dressing stick can be made from a wire coat hanger by pulling the triangular form into a long, thin handle. Use the hook part as you would use your dressing stick. Be careful of the sharp end.

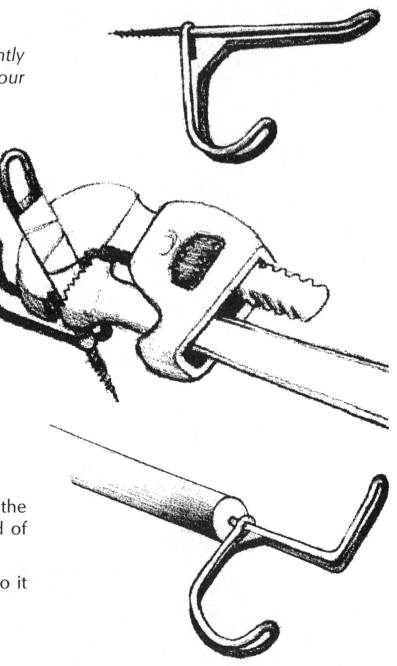

SHOE AND BOOT JACK

A boot jack is a very sensible device to have around the house. It is also a very old gadget — boot jacks can be found in museums and antique stores.

Some people get dizzy when they bend over to pull their shoes on or off. This simple device will be very useful for them. It can be a simple beginner's wood project.

If the boot jack is for a person who wears very large shoes, make it out of wider lumber and cut a deeper "V".

Directions:

1. Measure, mark, and cut the wood as shown in the illustration.

2. Sand well, rounding the sharp edges and points and edges of the "V" (as shown in the picture) to avoid ripping rubber boots on a sharp wooden edge.

3. Assemble as shown, using glue or screws.

4. Paint or polyurethane as desired.

You will need:

1 12"-long piece of 1" x 6" lumber
   (finished size ¾" x 5½")
1 5½"-long piece of 1" x 2" lumber
   (finished size ¾" x 1½")
white glue and/or two #8 x 1¼" flathead wood screws
sandpaper
polyurethane or paint (if desired)

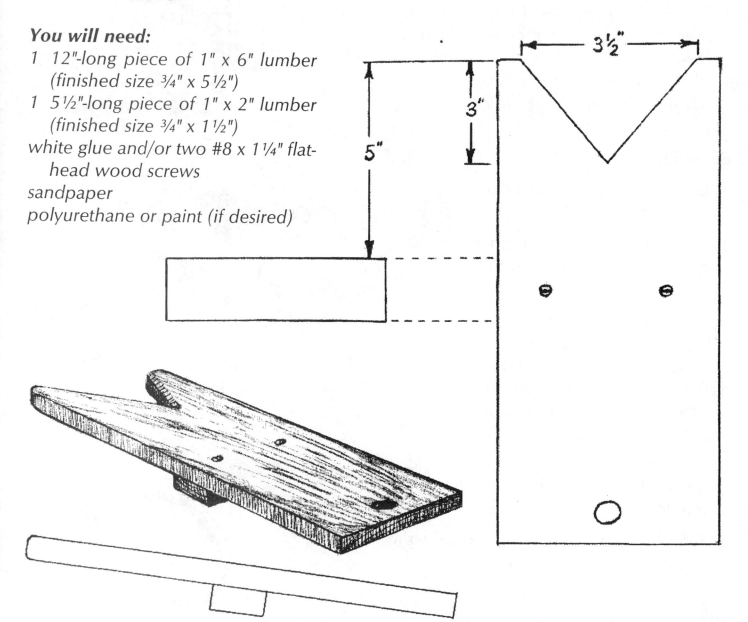

HAVE YOU THOUGHT ABOUT THIS?

Bedroom

- Keep a flashlight near your bed. Have several night lights in the room, and use light switches that glow in the dark or have internal lights.

- It is a good idea to have a light switch near the bedroom doorway, so you can turn on the light as you enter the room. For security, some people like to have a light switch in their bedroom that turns on lights outside the house.

- There should be a telephone near your bed. Don't use a wall phone. Choose a phone that can be pulled down to the floor in case you fall and need to call for help.

- There should be a lamp or switch that is reachable from your bed, so you don't have to get up to turn it on. Try a lamp that turns on with a touch or a clap. Regular table lamps can be changed to "touch" lamps with an adapter that screws into the light-bulb socket.

- Keep a commode chair or urinal in your bedroom for use at night so you don't have to make trips to the bathroom when you are sleepy and it's dark in the house.

- If you have weakness in your legs, make or purchase a simple "stirrup" leg-lifter (a loop you place on your foot with a long handle) to lift your leg onto a wheelchair or bed.

- Placement of furniture in the bedroom is important, especially if you're unsteady on your feet. Make sure that you have plenty of space to maneuver, and make sure that all pieces of furniture are strong and sturdy if you will need to hold onto them for a bit of support when you are walking around.

- Don't use throw rugs, and don't use extension cords that cross passageways.

- If your dog sleeps in your bedroom, give it a bed out of the way so you don't fall over your pet in the dark.

- There should be adequate electrical wiring and outlets in your bedroom. If possible, outlets should be a few feet above the floor to make them more accessible. It's a good idea to have outlets on each side of your bed, for your alarm clock, electric blanket, etc.

Dressing

- Getting up and getting dressed can be time-consuming, but psychologically, it is probably better for you than staying in your bathrobe all day. And getting dressed may even be a good "range of motion" exercise for you.

- Organizing your clothing ahead of time will save your energy. Lay out your clothes on a nearby chair or chest, ready for the next morning, so you don't have to hunt for them.

- If you're having difficulty getting dressed and undressed, consult with an occupational therapist for some advice. Undressing yourself is usually easier than dressing yourself; even if you need help getting dressed, you may be able to take your clothes off on your own.

- If one arm is weaker than the other, first put your weaker arm into a shirt or coat sleeve by guiding it completely in with your stronger arm. Then put your stronger arm into its sleeve. When you remove your shirt, take your stronger arm out of its sleeve first. With pants, put your weaker leg in first, pull that pants leg all the way on, and then put your stronger leg in.

- Dust your legs with talcum powder to make pulling on pantyhose easier.

- Reaching behind your back to close your bra can be a challenge. There are many bras available that fasten in the front. You can also fasten your regular bra around your waist in front of you, then turn the bra around and slip your shoulder straps on. Or perhaps a sports bra that slips on without any closure may be right for you.

- It's easier to put on sportswear like sweat suits with elastic waistbands than regular pants. Sweatpants are also washable and comfortable. Clothing that is one size larger than you usually wear may be easier to put on than a snugly fitting garment.

- When you're putting on shoes, instead of bending all the way to the floor, elevate your leg or prop your foot on a chair. You can get dizzy bending all the way over to put your shoe on.

- Put your belt through the belt loops before you put on your trousers.

- There are several specialty clothing catalogs (J.C. Penney, for example; see the Resources section). Clothing pattern makers like Simplicity have special booklets with instructions for making clothing to your own specifications.

SOME COMMERCIALLY AVAILABLE PRODUCTS

Here are some items available through specialty catalogs that you may find helpful for dressing.

- **Buttonhooks** are available in many styles. They're simple devices made of wire bent into a loop, with a handle. They help you button your clothing with one hand.

- **Long shoehorns** can help you to put on your shoes without having to bend down.

- **Sock aids** are devices to help you put on socks, stockings, and pantyhose without bending over. There are many styles on the market. You may find that one type works better for you than another.

- **Shoelace replacements** can be used if you can't tie your shoes. There are all sorts of shoelace replacements and modified shoe closings that will enable you to put on your shoes without having to tie the laces. Don't forget that many styles of shoes are available with Velcro closures. Slip-on shoes, too, may be an option.

- **Capes and ponchos** are handy if you use a wheelchair and go outside in bad weather. There are also specially designed outer garments for wheelchair users.

- **Long-reaching zipper pulls** are available for use with garments that fasten in the back.

- **Zipper boot inserts** allow you to wear high-top work boots or high-top sneakers without lacing them up. You lace the inserts permanently into your boots, and then you can just zip the boots closed. Redwing Work Shoes (a popular line of work boots sold in many stores) carries them in their catalog; they can also be found in Army and Navy surplus stores, or in the fireman's supply catalog listed in the Resources section.

CAREGIVER NOTES

- Bedrooms often contain a lifetime accumulation of belongings and memorabilia. Sometimes it's easy for us, as concerned caregivers, to say that the "clutter" should be cleaned up. Many times, our suggestion is not well received. Of course, if an older person has begun to use a wheelchair, then some rearranging and clearing out may be necessary whether or not it's received happily, because wheelchairs need a lot of room to maneuver.

- If an older person is walking independently, or with a cane, clutter is not as hazardous. Sometimes it can even be helpful — if some of the "clutter" is furniture that can provide a bit of support as a person passes by. Lightly holding on to a dresser, then to a sturdy chair, and then to the footboard of the bed can be reassuring to a person moving unsteadily in familiar territory. Do try, however, to remove scatter rugs, extension cords, and other things that can be tripped over.

- Sometimes removing accumulated belongings can be made more palatable if the items can be used by needy families, or by grandchildren moving out on their own. Being a giver of household items rather than a recipient of assistance can be a very strong motivator, especially at a time when there is a sense that personal independence is being lost.

- Nights can be hazardous because many older people get up frequently at night to go to the bathroom, groggily making their way to the bathroom in the dark. A commode chair in the bedroom can be of real assistance because it spares an older person from having to make repeated trips to the bathroom.

- If you are close by at night and you worry about being able to hear an older person who may need help, consider buying a nursery monitor, readily available in infant supply departments. Placing a monitor on the bedside table, or hung out of the way above the bed, will enable you to hear quiet calls for assistance even if you are at some distance from the bedroom.

C H A P T E R

Kitchen & Meal Time

3

REFRIGERATOR MODIFICATIONS

If you're purchasing a new refrigerator, choose a frost-free model that has sliding shelves. Select a style that is comfortable for you. For example, if you have problems with bending, you probably want to buy a refrigerator with a freezer on top. If you use a wheelchair, a "side-by-side" or a refrigerator with a bottom freezer may be more convenient.

If you're keeping your old refrigerator, however, these modifications will make it easier to use.

- To make the door easier to open, tie a loop of ribbon or stout rope around the door handle. Then you can slip your forearm through the loop and pull the door open.

- Plastic bags are great refrigerator storage containers, but twist-ties and zip-lock bags can be difficult to handle. Instead, fold over the end of a plastic bag several times and use a spring clothes-pin to keep the bag sealed. (You can avoid using your fingers to open the clothespin—rest the clothespin on its side on the counter and press it open with the palm of your hand.)

- Use inexpensive plastic trays or baskets to hold groups of small food containers such as jellies or condiments. Instead of looking for a single inconspicuous item tucked in among other things, you can slide the entire basket in and out of the refrigerator.

- Large containers of milk or juice can be difficult to lift and remove from the refrigerator. Inexpensive handles are available for these cartons.

- Instead of storing large containers of food or drink in the refrigerator, transfer the contents into smaller, lightweight containers.

- When you do have to remove a large or heavy container from the refrigerator, rest the container's weight on your forearm (with your elbow bent), and use your other hand only to steady the container, not to support it.

- Put a Lazy Susan on one of the refrigerator shelves. This will make it easier to get items that tend to "disappear" in the back of the shelf.

KITCHEN SINK MODIFICATIONS

Your kitchen sink may be too high or too low for your comfort, and the faucets may be difficult to operate as well. Here are some suggestions for making your kitchen sink more convenient for you.

- If you sit down when you are using the sink, or if you use a wheelchair, you want to have enough knee space under the sink so you can comfortably sit and work. (Wrap the sink drain pipe with foam pipe insulation so you won't bump or burn your legs when you're sitting at the sink.)

  The area under the sink can be modified to create this extra knee room (see picture). The kickboards, the center post, and the inside base of the under-sink cabinet have to be removed.

  Re-attach the center post and kickboards as shown in the picture.

  Notice in the picture that there are large, easy-to-grasp D-shaped cabinet door handles.

  After the kickboard, center post and inside base of the under-sink cabinet have been removed, rather than modify the cabinet doors, you can remove them and hang a cloth or bamboo curtain under the sink instead.

- If you are purchasing new sink hardware, the best kind of faucet handle to buy—the easiest kind to use—is a "single stick" or "single lever."

• Your sink is the right height for you if you can place your hands flat on the bottom of the sink basin without having to bend over. If your sink's basin is too deep, you can place a small dishpan or dish rack upside down in the sink to elevate dishes while you're washing them.

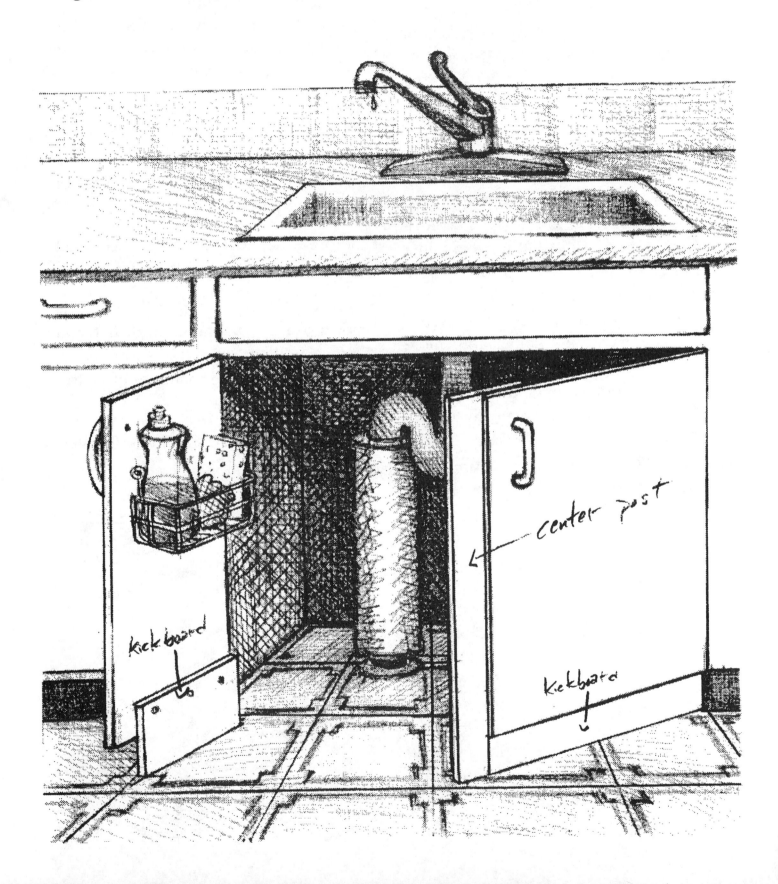

ADJUSTING YOUR HOT WATER TEMPERATURE

Water that is hotter than 120 degrees can cause scalds in a matter of seconds. At your tap, the hot water temperature should be less than 110 degrees Fahrenheit. Set your water heater to "LOW" or to 110 degrees.

If you don't know what your hot water temperature is, you can get an approximate measurement with a simple thermometer test at your sink. Take an inexpensive weather thermometer and put it in a small container in your sink. Fill the container with hot tap water and keep running the hot water over the thermometer until its indicator stops moving. If you see that the temperature at your hot water tap is more than 110 degrees, lower the temperature control at your hot water heater and try the thermometer test again the next day. (**Note:** This is a solution for private residences, not institutions. Remember, too, that the lower temperature may not be hot enough for your dishwasher.)

If you are unfamiliar with the controls of your water heater, ask a qualified person to adjust the temperature for you. If your landlord controls your hot water system, ask the landlord to consider lowering the temperature. If you can't adjust the water temperature at your water heater, consider installing anti-scald devices at the shower head and sink faucets. Ask for them at a plumbing store. The address of one manufacturer, Resources Conservation Company, is listed in the Resources section.

COOKING SAFETY

Cooking can be hazardous because of the heat and the risk of spilling hot food, boiling liquids, or cooking oil. Above all, be aware of the hazards around a stove and be as careful as you can.

- If you cook while you are seated in a wheelchair or on a stool, you must be particularly cautious because you can't move out of the way quickly in case of an accidental spill.

- Before you move a pan of hot food from the stove top, let it cool a bit.

- Before you move a pan, make sure it is not too heavy to move, and that you can securely grasp it. If it is too heavy, remove some of the contents before trying to move the pan.

- A fire extinguisher should be located

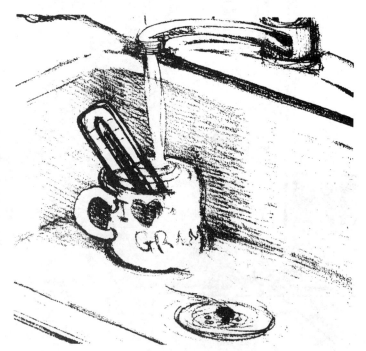

next to the stove, together with an easily accessible container of baking soda to put out grease fires.

- If there is anything hot on the stove, do not use a reacher to get things out of a cabinet located over the stove. If you dropped the reacher or the item, it could fall into a hot pot.

- Use good pot holders or cooking mitts to move pans.

- If you can, *slide* pans to a countertop or trivet so you don't have to lift them.

- Plan ahead. Know where you're going to put a hot pot *before* you pick it up. Use a bread board or cutting board near the stove as a trivet.

- Don't wear loose long-sleeved garments while you're cooking. Roll up your sleeves and hold them in place with rubber bands.

- Use a whistling teapot if you tend to forget that you've left the water on to boil.

- Fatigue contributes to cooking accidents. Save your energy by sitting to prepare your food whenever possible, using a rolling kitchen cart to hold your supplies, and using lightweight kitchen implements.

KITCHEN STOVES

Whether or not you do a lot of cooking, and even if you use a microwave oven, your kitchen range is still an important appliance. We prefer to see you use a microwave oven, toaster oven, or crock pot—but we know that many people do prefer to use their kitchen range. If you are one of those people, make your kitchen range easier and safer to use by following these guidelines.

- Use an electric range if possible. If you must use a gas range, install a gas alarm, which works like a smoke alarm to detect gas leaks or burners that are left open. Inquire at your local gas company.

- If you must use a match to light your oven, use a long barbecue match. These matches are about 12" long, so you won't have to bend as far to light your oven. You can reuse the match several times by relighting it from the stove burner. You can also use a spark-type barbecue lighter instead of a match.

- Range knobs can be hard to turn. Drill two small holes through a short piece of dowel and into the range knob. Fasten the dowel to the knob with screws, as shown in the illustration. Or drill a ¼" hole through the knob and push a short piece of ¼" dowel through the hole. You can also build up the knobs with epoxy putty (see p. 62), mixed, kneaded, and formed into a graspable shape on the existing stove knob.

- Mark the "OFF" position on the control

knob and on the range with a contrasting color. Use stove touch-up paint, available at a hardware store. (Nail polish can be used if your range's control panel doesn't get too hot.) If you can't read the numbers on your oven temperature setting knob, mark both the knob and the range at the temperature at which you usually use the oven (for example, at 350 degrees).

- If you buy a new range, make sure you can reach and manipulate the controls.

- If you cook using one hand, keep a filled teakettle on the rangetop. As shown in the picture, you can stabilize a saucepan handle against the teakettle while you stir the food in the saucepan.

- If you use a wheelchair, hang an unbreakable mirror (found in toy stores or auto supply stores)

at an angle above the stove so you can look down into pots on the stovetop. If you can't find an unbreakable mirror, carefully hang a glass mirror at an angle over the stove, as shown here.

ONE-HANDED CUTTING BOARD

This cutting board is for people who use only one hand to prepare food. The cutting board has a pair of stainless steel prongs to hold food in place for slicing or peeling, and a raised edge in one corner to hold bread in position for sandwich making. Accompanied by an easy-grip vegetable peeler or other useful kitchen gadget, this cutting board makes a nice gift.

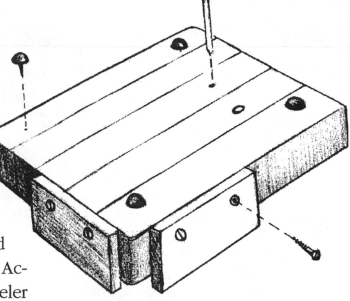

You will need:

1 small cutting board with straight edges, **or** 1 piece of maple or other hardwood, approximately 10" x 14" x ¾"

2 stainless steel nails, stainless steel screws with the threads ground off, or aluminum nails

2 strips of maple or other hardwood, approximately 1¼" x 4" x ½"

4 small flathead wood screws
vegetable oil

4 small rubber-tipped feet with tack ends (optional)

Directions:

1. If you are using a hardwood board, sand it smooth.

2. Drill two holes slightly smaller than the diameter of your stainless steel or aluminum nails or screws, and hammer them in from the underside of the cutting board so that they protrude (as shown in the illustration).

3. Cut and sand the two hardwood strips for the corner. Glue and screw them in place as shown.

4. Seal the wood strips with vegetable oil. If you are using a hardwood board, seal it with vegetable oil as well.

5. On the underside of the cutting board, drill four pilot holes for the nonslip feet. Tap the feet into place. (Silicone bathtub and tile sealant can be used instead of feet for a nonslip bottom; see p. 43 for instructions.)

This cutting board should not be washed in a dishwasher.

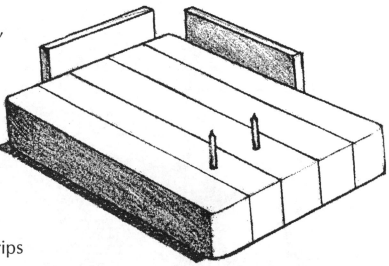

GROCERY BAG HANDLES

Plastic grocery bags have their good and bad points. If you have arthritis in your hands, or weak fingers, you may find it difficult or uncomfortable to carry your grocery bags by the plastic handles. These simple grocery bag handles may be very helpful. The handles can be stored in your handbag or fanny pack when they are not being used. A set of two handles, perhaps with one of each type of handle, would make a nice gift.

One-Hook Handle

You will need:
1 large cup hook (1"), **or** 1 large safety cup hook plus one wooden bead
1 4"-long piece of ¾" dowel
1 4" piece of foam hot-water-pipe insulation to fit over the dowel
plastic tape to wrap

Directions:

1. Drill a pilot hole in the middle of the dowel.

2. Screw in the cup hook so that the hook opens at right angles to the length of the dowel.

3. Split the foam pipe insulation and slip it over the dowel and hook as shown.

4. Wrap snugly with plastic tape.

5. To make a safety cup hook easier to open, use epoxy or other strong cement to glue a bead on the end of each cup hook spring (as shown on the next page in the illustration of the two-hook handle).

Two-Hook Handle

You will need:
2 large cup hooks (1"), **or** 2 large safety cup hooks plus 2 large beads
1 6"-long piece of ¾" dowel
1 6" piece of foam hot-water-pipe insulation to fit over the dowel
plastic tape to wrap

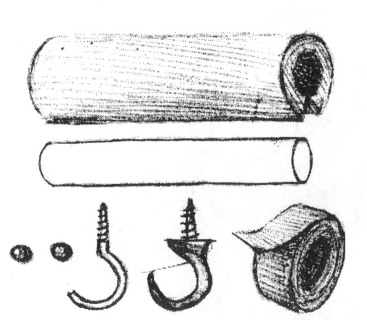

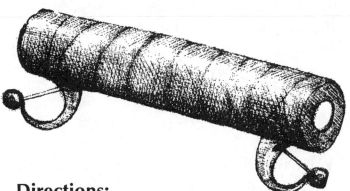

HIGH-WALL AND NONSLIP DISHES

Medical specialty catalogs have lots of special dishes for people who have trouble getting their food onto a fork or spoon. These dishes can be quite expensive, and there are several inexpensive alternatives that often work just as well.

Look for a single-serving ovenware casserole or microwave bowl with sides that are almost vertical. This type of bowl works well as a high-wall dish. To keep the dish from sliding on the table, use a placemat-sized piece of nonslip plastic shelf lining, a wonderful product now widely available in stores. Or you can try this simple modification to the dish itself:

Directions:

1. Drill two pilot holes in the dowel, positioned ¾" from each end as shown.

2. Screw in the cup hooks so that they open toward the ends of the dowel.

3. Split the foam insulation and slip it over the dowel and hooks as shown.

4. Wrap snugly with plastic tape.

5. To make safety cup hooks easier to open, use epoxy or other strong cement to glue a bead on the end of each cup hook spring (as shown here).

1. Apply a small amount of silicone bathtub and tile sealant around the bottom of the bowl.

2. Moisten your finger in water. Smooth out the bead of silicone lightly with your finger.

3. Set the bowl down to dry, right-side-up, on a piece of plastic wrap or plastic trash bag.

4. After 24 hours, when the silicone caulking is dry, peel off the plastic wrap, and you'll have a bowl that won't slip on the tabletop. (Don't wash this bowl in a dishwasher or use it in a microwave oven.)

BUILT-UP SILVERWARE

There are many kinds of special kitchen utensils, including silverware, available through specialty catalogs. Some of these utensils have built-up handles. If you're going to use special utensils for a long time, it's a good idea to buy ready-made ones because they are easier to keep clean. However, if you only need easy-to-grasp silverware for a short period of time, or if you want to see if built-up silverware works for you, try this inexpensive, homemade alternative.

Your physical or occupational therapist can give you some foam rubber tubing the right size for silverware handles, or you can use hot-water-pipe insulation with a lengthwise wedge cut out of it, as shown in the picture.

Directions:

1. Cut a 3½" length of foam pipe insulation (3" for teaspoons).

2. Cut a lengthwise strip out of the insulation. This will make the tubing smaller in diameter, so it is easier to grasp and will fit the silverware better.

3. Slip the insulation over the end of the utensil handle, and wrap it tightly with plastic tape. The silverware should not turn inside the tubing. If it does, undo the tape and cut another lengthwise strip from the insulation.

Wash these utensils only by hand, not in a dishwasher.

You can also use a piece of terrycloth or washcloth to make a built-up handle in the same way suggested for a built-up toothbrush handle (shown in Chapter 1, p. 9). The advantage of a cloth handle is that it can be laundered regularly.

MEALTIME APRON

A more attractive mealtime solution than an adult bib, this apron—made from a piece of vinyl tablecloth—can be wiped clean or machine washed. (Don't put it in the dryer.) Several aprons can usually be made from one tablecloth. An inexpensive tablecloth is less stiff than an expensive one, so it's more suitable for this project.

The pattern shown will fit most people. If the apron is for a very large person, make the pattern pieces bigger at the fold lines. The apron will tuck nicely around your lap. It is meant to be worn while sitting, so there are no ties at the waistline.

This apron may be difficult for you to put on by yourself. If you are going to put it on by yourself, cut the neck hole bigger so you can slip the apron on over your head, and sew both ends of the strap to the apron instead of using Velcro.

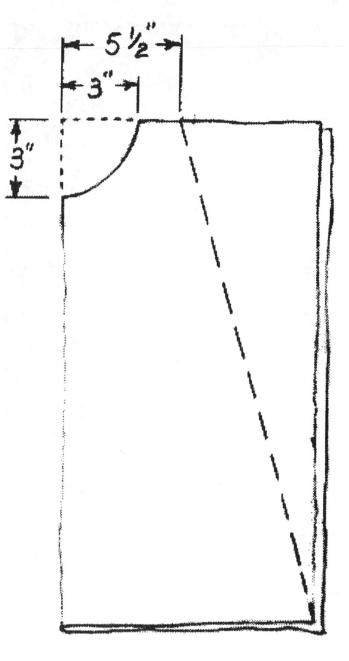

You will need:

1 inexpensive, vinyl, flannel-backed table-cloth

1 two-part 3" piece of ½"-wide Velcro sew-on tape (3" hook part, 3" loop part)

Directions:

1. Fold a large sheet of newspaper in half and sketch the pattern on it as shown here, taking care to accurately copy the shoulder dimensions. Trace the apron strap pattern from the next page on another folded piece of newspaper, matching the "Fold" line to the fold in the paper so that the resulting pattern is doubled. (If the pattern needs to be made larger, add 1" extra width along the fold line on both the apron pattern piece and the apron strap fold line.) Cut the pattern pieces out.

2. Open the patterns and lay them flat on the tablecloth. Lightly tape the pattern pieces to the vinyl so they don't slip. Cut out the apron and apron strap.

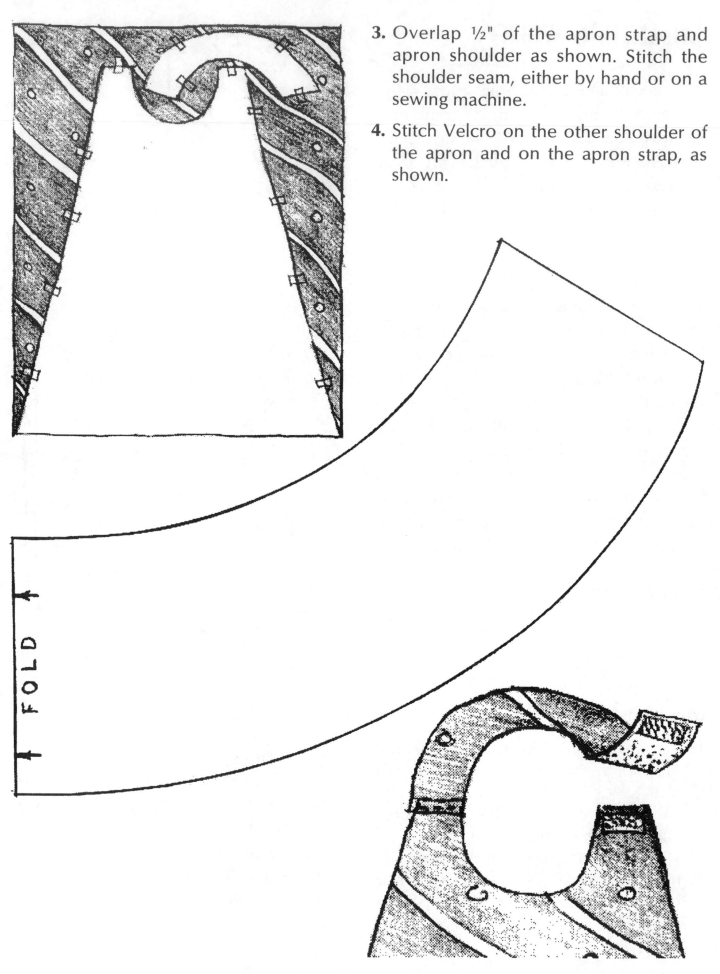

3. Overlap ½" of the apron strap and apron shoulder as shown. Stitch the shoulder seam, either by hand or on a sewing machine.

4. Stitch Velcro on the other shoulder of the apron and on the apron strap, as shown.

FOLD

DINING SMOCK

If you need to protect your clothing when you eat, but you are self-conscious about wearing a "bib" in public, you may like this dining smock, invented by an Iowa woman for her husband. It will work just as well for a woman. You simply slip your arms into the sleeves and fasten it in back. Wear the smock over your shirt or dress and spread a cloth napkin on your lap. You will probably need someone to help you put this smock on.

The woman who thought of this idea suggested buying inexpensive, dark-colored shirts at a used clothing store. It is easier to cut straight down the back if the shirt is striped or plaid.

You will need:

1 used shirt or blouse, one size larger than normal

1 strip of Velcro (both hook and loop parts), ⅝" wide and 4" long

Directions:

1. Button the shirt up the front, and cut the shirt down the center of the back, through the collar, the yoke, and the length of the back.

2. Overcast the raw edges by hand or sewing machine, sewing through all thicknesses of the folded collar, as shown.

3. Sew on the Velcro fastener tape as shown in the picture on the next page. Sew the rough "hook" part of the Velcro on the right side of the shirt (so it can't rub on your skin). Don't put Velcro further down the shirt, since you will be seated while eating.

4. If you want the cuffs to be easy to slip on and off without undoing buttons, enlarge the cuff opening by using elastic thread or ponytail holders (as shown in Chapter 2, p. 27), and leave the cuff buttons permanently fastened.

BACK VIEW

You can make the shirt stain-resistant by spraying the front with Scotchgard fabric protector (automobile supply stores carry this product for car upholstery fabric). Or you can launder the shirt after each use and discard it when it becomes stained.

A cloth napkin draped on your lap will conceal the shirt-tails. You can sew a fabric napkin permanently to the shirt front at lap level. A sewn-on napkin may be more effective in keeping spills off your pants or skirts.

HAVE YOU THOUGHT ABOUT THIS?

- Use storage space efficiently. Install shallow utility drawers (underneath counters), sliding baskets, shelves, hangers, or Lazy Susans. If you have problems with your fingers or hands, use dividers to create vertical filing/storage areas to keep dishes, pans, casseroles, etc. stored upright. You can get a dish or pan out of a vertical rack by grasping it between your palms instead of having to hold it with your fingers.

- Create activity centers. For example, set up an area where you can comfortably prepare your ingredients for cooking. Have a work surface the right height for you. Keep a chair or stool there; an office-type swivel chair without arms is often a good choice. Have all the supplies you might need within easy reach, even if this means keeping duplicates of some kitchen utensils or seasonings. Keep in mind your right- or left-handedness when arranging the spaces.

- Put well-anchored grab bars at handy places such as the doorway of the kitchen. Mount a large D-shaped door handle on the side of your counter top or elsewhere to steady yourself. You may get dizzy when you are reaching upward for an item or when you are tilting your head back. Having a grab bar or handle to hold may help you keep your balance.

- To stabilize a mixing bowl, hold it on your lap, or set the bowl in a drawer and shut the drawer against the bowl—leaning against the drawer to keep pressure on the bowl's side, which prevents the bowl from rotating as you stir or beat the ingredients in it. To keep your mixing bowl, cutting board, or other kitchen utensil from sliding on a counter, use a piece of nonslip rug backing or nonslip shelf-lining (sold in many stores). Even a damp cloth spread out on your counter will provide some slip resistance.

- A microwave oven can be wonderful, but make sure that you place it at a good height, keeping in mind that you will be handling hot foods. As with other ovens, there should be space right next to the microwave oven in case you need to set something down in a hurry. Make sure you can see and manipulate the oven's controls easily. If you work sitting down, put the microwave oven on a table with open knee space underneath so you can work comfortably.

- Drawer and cabinet pulls can be changed to D-shaped handles for easy gripping. Mount D-shaped handles on your dishwasher door for easier opening. Instead of using your hand, put a loop made out of stout rope or webbing on drawers or sliding doors. Slip your forearm through the loop to pull open the drawer or door.

SOME COMMERCIALLY AVAILABLE PRODUCTS

There are probably more kitchen- and eating-related adaptive devices than any other kind. If you can, talk with an occupational therapist about helpful kitchen gadgets. Or look in a specialty catalog.

Other good sources of adaptive equipment are the many mail-order catalogs that come before Christmas. You'll be surprised at how many of the "labor-saving" devices shown in those catalogs can be helpful to you.

- Milk carton holders, plastic bag and box top openers, and many other kinds of convenient kitchen aids are available from specialty and regular mail-order catalogs. Do comparison shopping in several catalogs.

- Kitchen timers with large digital numbers and large control buttons are available in many kitchenware departments.

- Swedish knives are available in specialty catalogs. They are designed with angled handles that let your arm work in a natural, relaxed position (you need to use ⅕ as much force as with a regular knife.) There are several sizes and styles available.

- Doing your kitchen work one-handed? Install a kitchen scrub brush with a suction-cup base in or near your sink to wash dishes with one hand. Install a manual or electric jar opener (many styles are available in specialty catalogs) on the underside of your overhead cabinet. Many styles of jar opening devices are also available for two-handed use. (Sometimes just wrapping a wide rubber band around a stubborn jar lid will improve your grip enough to open the jar.)

- Electric can openers can be very helpful, but make sure you purchase a model with controls that you can handle comfortably. There are also some manual can openers that are gear-driven and easy to use.

- "Universal design" kitchen utensils are now available in many stores' kitchenware departments. These utensils have soft, comfortable hand grips, and mechanisms that are designed to work well for everybody.

- Knob turners will work on any non-round control knob or appliance handle. Although you could probably modify each and every knob in the house, a single portable knob turner will work on most of them.

- A wheeled kitchen utility cart can be used to move items around the room. If your kitchen isn't located near the entrance to your house, use the utility cart to move your groceries from the front door to your kitchen.

- Cutting food can be done with a regular knife, but there are other options if you find a kitchen knife hard to use. Sharp kitchen scissors can be used to cut meat or even sandwiches. Pizza cutters have round, sharp, stainless steel blades and make excellent roller knives to use instead of a regular knife.

- There are very attractive styles of drinking cups, glasses, and stemware designed for people with grasping problems. There are many types of high-wall dishes and dinnerware sets, and attractive silverware with handles that are easy to grasp. In the case of dinnerware, "special" does not have to mean unattractive. Shop in the specialty catalogs for pleasing, useful eating and cooking implements.

CAREGIVER NOTES

- A meal center can be created if an older person cannot use the range or household refrigerator. A small table (even a sturdy card table), with a small microwave oven and a small refrigerator within reach, are all that is necessary to create a "lunch nook" where an older person can prepare a hot beverage or meal independently. If the person cannot reach the sink, plastic water containers with easy-to-use spigots can be kept in the refrigerator for fresh drinking water. Set up the center for wheelchair accessibility if appropriate, or with a sturdy chair. Make sure there is adequate lighting.

- If you are purchasing kitchen utensils or appliances for a person with limited hand strength or movement, try the controls yourself with your fist closed and with light pressure. If you have trouble using the controls, the person for whom you are buying the appliance may have trouble as well.

- Safety is of paramount concern in the kitchen. Look at the "Cooking Safety" section (p. 38) and make sure there are, in fact, functioning fire extinguishers, smoke alarms and carbon monoxide alarms. Also inquire about a gas alarm (it will sound an alarm if someone turns the gas on but forgets to light the burner on a gas range) at your local gas utility company.

- To prevent falls, make sure there is a convenient and sturdy stepstool near the overhead cupboards. Try to arrange things so that frequently used items are easy to reach. Strips of wood can be nailed down along high shelves (halfway back) to keep objects from "wandering" to the back and becoming hard to reach. It's best to keep frequently used items on a lower, reachable location.

- Use a swivel desk chair with lockable casters to get an older person close to the kitchen table for meals. You can select a chair with or without arms.

- If you are remodeling the kitchen, evaluate the height and placement of furnishings and appliances carefully, because several, very differently sized or shaped people may need to work in the kitchen at different times.

C H A P T E R

Living Room & Leisure Activities

RAISING AN ARMCHAIR OR SOFA

It can be hard to get up out of an old comfortable armchair when the seat is low. If you use a wheelchair, getting in and out of a low armchair may be nearly impossible. Raising the height of the armchair's seat is often the solution. Most people find a seat height of 18" or 19" best. Sometimes putting a pillow under the seat cushion raises the height just enough. Depending on the present height of your armchair seat, you can raise an armchair simply by combining different sizes of stock lumber. This solution will work for a sofa as well.

You will need:
lumber, as follows:
- *To raise a chair two inches, use 2" x 2" and 1" x 4" lumber*
- *To raise a chair three inches, use 2" x 3" and 1" x 5" lumber*
- *To raise a chair four inches, use 2" x 4" and 1" x 6" lumber*

1   sheet of ⅝" plywood
24 3" or 3½" wood screws
polyurethane, stain, or paint (if desired)

The following instructions are written for raising a chair four inches. To raise the chair two inches or three inches, simply use another size of lumber.

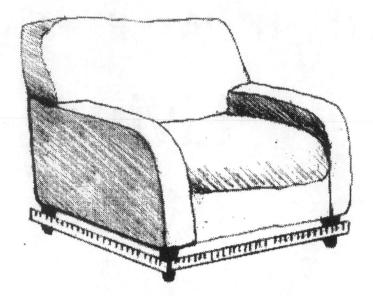

Directions:

1. Turn your armchair over on its side. Regardless of how much you want to raise the chair, measure the outside dimensions of the chair 2" up from the bottom of the legs, as illustrated. Cut a rectangular piece of $^5/_8$" plywood to match these dimensions.

2. Cut two pieces of 2 x 4 to match the **length** of your plywood rectangle. Cut two pieces of 1 x 6 the same length.

3. Cut two pieces of 1 x 6 exactly the **width** of your plywood rectangle **plus 1½"** (to allow for the overlap).

4. Make a box as shown in the illustration. Because you are screwing into the end grain of your wood, you need to use long screws to attach the front and back pieces to the sides.

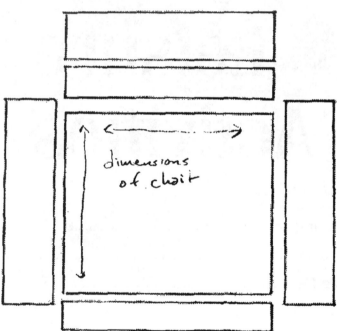

dimensions of chair

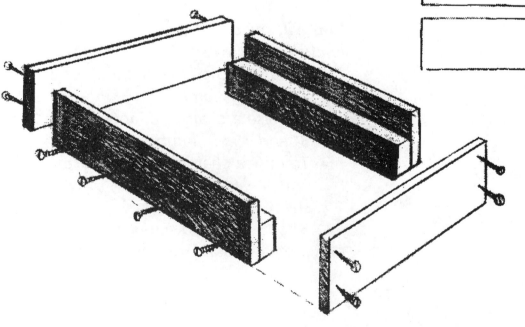

5. Set the plywood into the box and fasten with screws or nails.

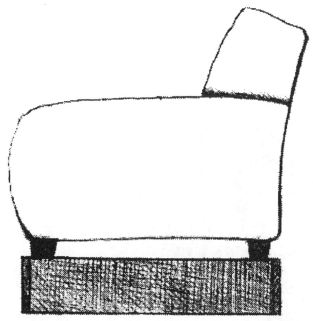

6. Apply stain or other finish as desired and set your chair in the box. For extra stability, screw the front legs of the chair to the platform.

Making the seat firmer will also help you get in and out of your chair. Insert a large square of scrap plywood underneath the seat cushion.

FOOTSTOOL

If you raise your armchair so that it is easier to get in and out of, you may find you need a footstool for your legs. Or you may just enjoy having your feet and legs elevated a bit.

This footstool is simple to make and very sturdy. You can change the dimensions to suit you. Take care, however, to keep the same general proportions to ensure stability. For example, if you raise the height, you should make the base wider also.

You will need:

1 piece of 1" x 10" (¾" x 9½" finished) lumber 36" long, for top and sides
1 piece of 1" x 4" (¾" x 3½" finished) lumber 11½" long, for stretcher (center piece)
1 piece of foam 9½ x 16 x 2"
1 piece of upholstery fabric 24 x 18"
8 #8 x 1½" flathead wood screws
staples or upholstery tacks
sandpaper
stain, polyurethane, or paint (if desired)

Directions:

1. Measure, mark, and cut the 1" x 10" into three pieces. The top piece is 16" long. The two leg pieces are each 10" long.

2. Using two screws on each end, assemble the two legs and the center piece.

3. Set the top in place and fasten with two screws into each leg.

4. Sand the stool and apply paint or finish.

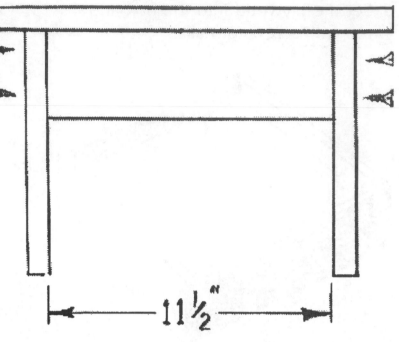

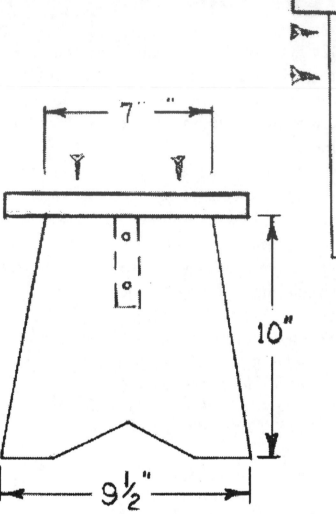

7"

10"

9½"

11½"

5. Glue the foam to the stool top.

6. Lay the fabric on a table (wrong side up). Place the stool upside down, centered on the fabric.

7. Working from one corner, stretch the fabric over the seat and staple or tack the edges on the underside of the stool top. Trim the excess fabric.

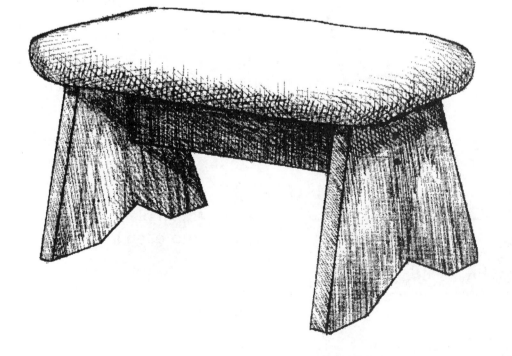

LAP DESK

A lap desk is a simple, portable work surface that rests across the arms of an arm chair. It is an old favorite; in many families, lap desks have been handed down through generations. If your family doesn't have one, start your own family heirloom. The lap desk can be personalized and decorated as a gift.

Before you begin, find a large piece of corrugated cardboard and cut out a prototype of the lap desk so you can determine the exact size lap desk to match your size and your chair. You should also measure the vertical distance from the chair seat to the top of the arms, to make sure there will be enough room for your legs under the lap desk when you sit in the chair.

You will need:
1 piece of ¼" luan (smooth-surfaced) plywood, 20 x 32" (approximate measurements depending on the arm chair)
silicone bathtub and tile sealant
stain, polyurethane, or paint

Directions:

1. Measure your chair and cut a rectangle of plywood 20" wide and 2" longer than the distance between the outer edges of your chair's arms (generally approximately 30" to 32").

2. Trace the pattern for the lap cut-out onto a folded sheet of newspaper. Cut out the pattern.

3. Find the midpoint on the plywood rectangle and lay the pattern on it with the fold at the midpoint. Trace around the pattern.

4. Using a jig saw, round the rectangle's corners, and cut out the lap cut-out. Cut hand holes if desired.

5. Sand all the rough edges; decorate and stain the lap desk.

6. To help keep the lap desk from sliding around, spread a thin coating of silicone bathtub and tile sealant on the underside of the lap desk where it will rest on the chair's arms.

CAUTION: This lap desk will not provide a stable surface for use by a person with spasticity or coordination problems. NEVER rest a cup of hot liquid on the lap desk.

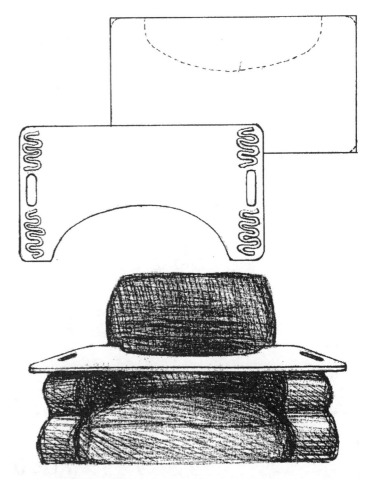

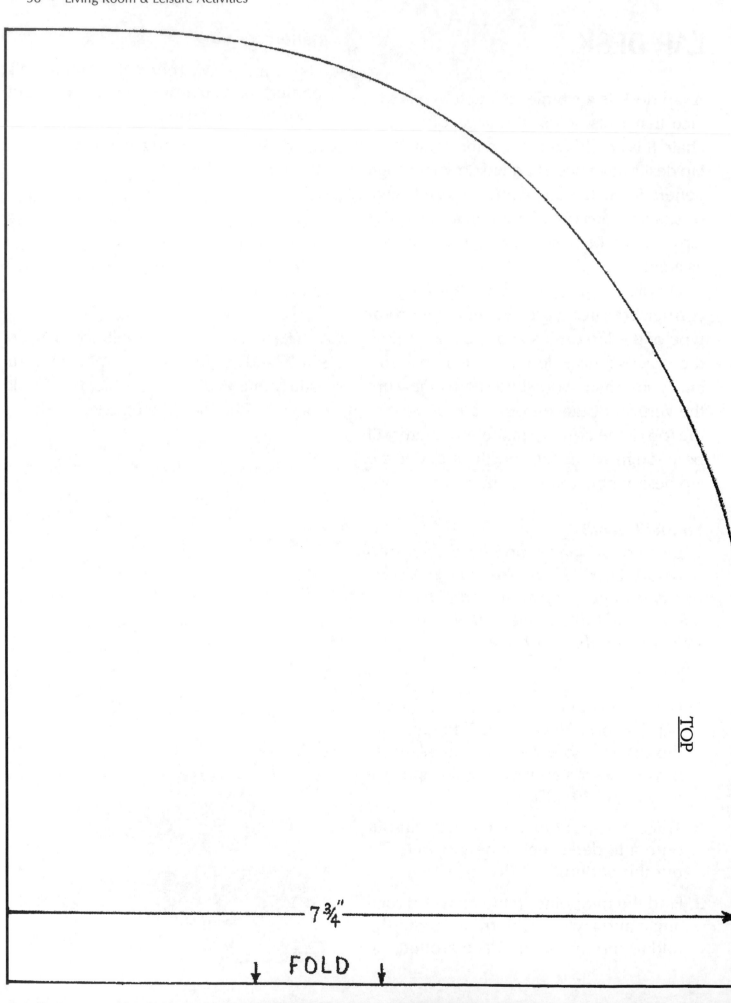

TOP

|← 7¾" →|

FOLD

UTILITY TRAY

This is an easy way to keep things organized, especially if small items are hard for you to hold on to, or slip easily out of your grasp. Keeping your things in a tray will keep them from falling off the side table and onto the floor. The tray can be decorated with paint, wallpaper, or contact paper to be given as a gift. A less elaborate tray can be made from a sturdy shallow cardboard box, but the project shown here will last for years.

Attach the handles near the top of the tray for easier grasping. Use handles that are easy to slip your hand through. The tray shown here is 11" x 14", but it can be made any size you want. Remember to make the sides long enough to overlap at the corners.

You will need:

1 11" x 14" piece of ¼" luan (smooth-surfaced) mahogany plywood
1 51" piece of lattice molding, 1¾" x ¼"
2 D-shaped cabinet door handles, with bolts
1 7" piece of quarter-round molding (either ½" or ¾" size) for the corners
sandpaper

carpenter's glue, plus small screws and brads if desired
polyurethane, paint, contact paper, and/or other decoration materials

Directions:

1. If your plywood has not been cut to size, cut it to 11" x 14".

2. Measure, mark, and cut two pieces of lattice each exactly 11" long, and two pieces of lattice exactly 14½" long.

3. Measure, mark, and cut four pieces of quarter-round molding, each 1¾" long.

4. Using glue, assemble the tray as shown in the picture. In each corner, glue the quarter-round molding as shown. If desired, make small pilot holes and reinforce the corners and bottom with small screws. Or use small brads to reinforce the corners and bottom of the tray.

5. Sand and finish. Decorate if desired.

6. Attach the handles near the top of the tray by drilling holes for the bolts. Be careful, since lattice molding splits easily.

ARMCHAIR CADDY

The armchair caddy is a convenient three-pocket "hold-all" that you can attach to the arm of your favorite upholstered chair. It can hold your reading glasses, TV guide, and remote control for your television. This is a simple sewing project and makes a nice gift. There's no cutting involved, only simple sewing.

You will need:
1 hand or dish towel, about 15" x 24"
sewing thread

Directions:

1. Fold the towel in half (as illustrated) with the decorated sides together. Then fold back one side so the hemmed edge lines up with the halfway fold. The double-folded part will form the pockets.

2. Pin the edges of the pockets and sew through all three layers of fabric along the two edges of the bag. Reinforce your stitching at the top of the pocket.

3. Sew two other parallel lines of stitching as shown in the drawing, dividing the pocket into three sections. (You may want to make the pockets of unequal sizes, depending on what you plan to put in them.) Reinforce your stitching at the tops of the middle seams.

The seams form three pockets. Depending on the style of your armchair, you can fasten the caddy to the arm of your chair with safety pins (tucked out of sight), or add extra fabric to the end of the towel to slide between the cushion and the chair arm.

HOW TO HAVE YOUR TV LOUD AND SOFT AT THE SAME TIME

If you have trouble hearing your television, but the loud TV volume bothers other people, you can purchase an amplification system at a home-electronics store. Or you can try this homemade solution.

You will need:

1 pair of small earphones

1 small, inexpensive black-and-white television set that has an earphone jack (You may be able to find a used TV that has a bad picture tube.)

Directions:

1. Set the small TV next to you. You don't have to have the screen in view, but the knobs must be within reach.

2. Plug the earphones into the earphone jack of the small TV. When you want to watch TV, turn both sets on, and turn the small set to the channel you are watching on your regular TV.

3. You can turn the volume on the little TV as loud as you want because you are listening with earphones. Your regular TV can be at a low volume for other watchers.

4. If having the small black-and-white TV picture on bothers or distracts you, turn the brightness adjustment so the picture is all dark. Or tape a piece of cardboard over the screen.

5. If you have cable service, get a cable splitter and some extra cable from an electronics store so the small television can receive the same channels as your regular TV.

Other ideas:

- Radios are available that tune into TV station frequencies. You can use earphones with this special kind of radio and turn it to the same channel you are watching on your regular TV. Be aware, however, that the dials on these radios are generally quite small, and the numbers can be hard to see.

- Check your local electronics store for remote headphones for TVs. You may find the price affordable.

KNOBS, DIALS, AND CONTROLS

Television control knobs, remote controls, and other controls for radios and the like can be made easier to use by making a few simple modifications.

- With typewriter correction fluid or bright-colored nail polish, paint some of the buttons to remind you what each button's function is. You might want to color the "on-off" switch with one color, for instance, and mark other buttons with a different color.

- Stick a small piece of adhesive tape to a button you use often, like the "on-off" switch. Or mark buttons with colored plastic tape, which is available at any variety store.

- Remote controls with large numbers are available and can be set for VCRs and TV sets.

- Build up a knob with epoxy putty, a two-colored material that you can buy in a hardware store. Break off a small chunk of each color, knead the two together until the color is uniform, and mold the putty around the knob you are modifying. The putty hardens at room temperature. (**Note:** You will not be able to remove this modification from the knob.)

- With epoxy glue, attach a short section of dowel to a knob that is hard to grasp. Or drill a small hole in both the knob and dowel, and attach the dowel with a small screw. (See the illustration for modifying stove knobs on pp. 39-40.)

- If you have a problem with a slippery knob, the solution may be as simple as winding a rubber band around the knob several times, increasing the size of the knob slightly and making it easier to grasp and turn.

- Commercially available knob turners can be purchased from specialty supply catalogs. These turners will work with a wide variety of handles, faucets, and dials, as well as irregularly-shaped knobs. Knob turners generally have large, easy-to-grasp handles, to help people who have limited use of their hands.

PLAYING CARD HOLDER

If you use only one hand, holding playing cards can be frustrating. The playing card holder on this page is a simple-to-make solution to this problem. If every player at the table uses a card holder, then nobody will feel different or singled out.

This set of four card holders makes a nice gift, accompanied by a deck of cards with large numbers. The holders can be decorated creatively with magic markers or paint.

You will need:

1 *4'-long piece of 1" x 2" lumber (finished size ¾" x 1½")*
1 *8'-long piece of ¾" quarter-round molding*
sandpaper
white glue
paint or polyurethane
magic markers, stencils, or other decorations

Directions:

1. Cut all the wood into 12" lengths. You'll have four pieces of the 1" x 2" and eight pieces of the quarter-round molding.

2. Glue two pieces of molding to each length of 1" x 2" as shown, leaving a slot in the middle.

3. Sand the rough edges, paint, and decorate the card holders as desired. To make the slot easier to see, you can paint the inner surfaces of the slot a darker, contrasting color.

HAVE YOU THOUGHT ABOUT THIS?

If you spend a lot of time in your living room every day, take a moment and look around. How can you make it more convenient, comfortable, and safe? Here are some suggestions:

- Think of your favorite easy chair as your "Control Center." Within reach around you, arrange good lighting and your favorite radio. Have a TV with a remote control (with large numbers) that you can operate. Make sure your TV is not reflecting glare from windows or lamps. Keep a sturdy table next to you for beverages, books, and magazines. Keep a telephone within reach for convenience and safety. A cordless phone can be very handy.

- Make the furniture in your living room hospitable for other people. Have a firm chair with arms for guests who have difficulty getting up or sitting down. Arrange the living room furniture so that a person in a wheelchair can be included comfortably in your circle of conversation. Make sure passageways are wide enough.

- Make sure that you have adequate lamps and lighting throughout the room, but also make sure there are no loose wires to trip over. If you are seated near a lamp, but its switch is not within reach, add a short extension cord with a roll switch so you can bring the lamp switch to within easy reaching distance. Or buy a "clap" or "touch" lamp, which can be turned on and off by clapping your hands or by touching the lamp base.

- If your window sill is no more than 30" from the floor, you will be able to sit in your chair and look out the window comfortably.

- If you have difficulty reading printed books, you can obtain books on tape for free from your state's Library Service for the Blind. Their address is listed in the Resources section. Ask also about other services like side-band radios.

- If a pencil, pen, or paintbrush is hard to hold, make a built-up grip from a small ball such as a Ping-Pong ball, a practice golf ball (the hollow plastic kind), or a 2" foam ball. Simply slip the pencil through the ball.

LEISURE-RELATED PRODUCTS AND SERVICES

- If your vision is impaired, you may want to try reading large-print books, available at your library or through your state library system. There are books on tape, Scrabble sets and playing cards with large print, self-threading needles, and a host of other recreation aids. Many newspapers and magazines put out large-print editions. Look in the Resources section for an agency that serves people with vision impairments, and call for information.

- If you are hard of hearing, there are various amplifying systems that you can use with your television. Closed captioning—which displays at the bottom of the screen the words that are spoken on the TV—can be very helpful. Many videotaped films with closed captioning are available for rental or purchase. For more information, look in the Resources section for the organization "Self Help for the Hard of Hearing" (SHHH).

- If you have physical problems, there are innumerable gadgets that may help you. These include book and newspaper holders, playing card holders, spring-operated scissors, devices that enable you to knit, crochet, or do needlework with one hand, and so on. Ask an occupational therapist for suggestions,

and look in the Resources section for the names of some of the specialty catalogs.

- For people who enjoy outdoor activities, the American Horticultural Therapy Association will direct your gardening questions to appropriate organizations. Look in the Resources section for their toll-free number and for the names of several books on gardening for people with disabilities. (See Chapter 6 for more suggestions on gardening.)

- Would-be travelers who need information about worldwide travel accessibility should contact:

Travel Information Center
Moss Rehabilitation Hospital
12th and Tabor Road
Philadelphia, PA 19141

CAREGIVER NOTES

A living room may become a combination of bedroom, lounge, visiting room, and day room. Perhaps a family member is coming home from the hospital and you want to use the living room as a temporary "convalescence" room. Or perhaps you are facing the temporary or permanent accessibility problems caused by upstairs bedrooms. The following hints can help make the room transformation easier.

- Living rooms are typically more public than bedrooms. That may mean having to pick things up quickly if guests are about to arrive, and living rooms tend not to have the same storage areas as bedrooms, which makes the picking up trickier. So try to come up with creative storage ideas. Move a dresser into the room. If there's a hall nearby, you can use it to store personal or convalescent equipment and supplies. A blanket chest or trunk used as a coffee table can also be used for storage.

- A wonderful idea is to create a daybed, using a tailored bedspread and adding throw pillows to create a sofa "look" during the day.

- Inexpensive wire storage shelves or steel utility shelves can be purchased from a discount store and placed in the living room or in the closet for extra storage space. In a pinch, plastic milk crates stacked on top of one another can provide shelf space. Wire shelf units for small items can be hung on the inside of the closet door.

- You may want to change from dark living room drapes to light, translucent cafe curtains to let in more light but still provide privacy. Additional lighting or rearrangement of lamps may help make the room brighter and more cheerful.

- A privacy screen can be erected to create a visual barrier to separate a more formal area from the part of the living room that is now a bedroom. This may be appreciated by your family member, especially if a commode chair has been placed near the bed. Furniture can be used to create walls, but make sure the furniture you use is stable enough to stand alone without falling.

- Hygiene is also a consideration, particularly around and under the bed. If the living room carpet may become stained, cover the floor under the bed or roll up the carpet.

- Bedside hints: If you are moving a TV so that it can be watched from the bed, make sure that it is set in a glare-free place so that light doesn't reflect off the screen. Install a lamp or light that can be safely turned on and off from bed. A bedside table for a book, clock, or beverage is important.

House-keeping & Getting Around

BASIC DIMENSIONS

Furniture, appliances, and dwellings seem to be created for "average" people. If you're not average-sized, it can be hard to do things even when you're young and flexible. As you get older and less agile, your body has more and more trouble adjusting to average-height work surfaces, average-width doorways, and average-sized steps. Maybe it's time to make your environment accommodate *your* body rather than the other way around.

You'll need to make some measurements to change your environment to fit. Use a flexible metal carpenter's rule, and get someone to help. If you use a wheelchair, take your measurements in your wheelchair.

In calculating maneuvering space, especially if you use a wheelchair, give yourself ample room. In any case, you'll want to answer the following questions:

- How low can you reach or bend?

- How far to the front and side can you reach?

- How high can you reach? (Measure not only when reaching straight overhead, but when reaching forward and up at the same time.)

- What is the best height and depth for stair steps?

Not all wheelchairs are average, either. Although 60" is a standard turning radius for a wheelchair, and 27" is a standard clearance for your knees, these measurements may not be right for you. If you use a wheelchair, consider the following questions:

- How far in front of the wheelchair do your feet extend?

- What is the comfortable clearance for your knees?

- What is your best work-surface height (clearing wheelchair and knees)?

- What is your comfortable turning radius?

- How narrow a passageway can you comfortably pass through?

Walkers require approximately 18" to 24" around and in front of them. Crutches require about 32" in width, and a person with a cane or one crutch requires about 25" to 27". But these are only estimates. You, yourself, must be measured.

Note: A friendly reminder to the carpenter/electrician doing the actual installation: Keep in mind the size of the person you're building for, not yourself, when you install wall switches and overhead handles.

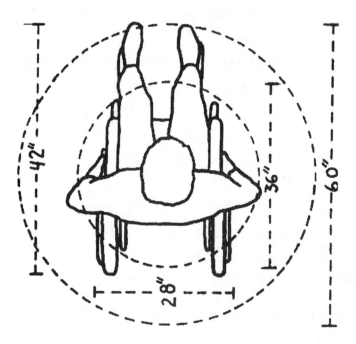

Some standard measurements for wheelchair users.

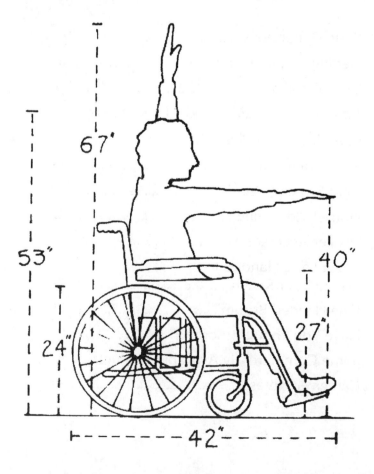

GETTING THROUGH DOORWAYS

If you use a wheelchair and a doorway in your house is a little too narrow for you to get through, there are a couple of changes you can make without going to any great expense. These changes may make the doorway wide enough for you to get through.

- Replace the conventional door hinges with offset hinges, which you can purchase at a building supply company. Using these hinges (shown in the inset illustration) adds about 1½" to the width of a doorway. This may be enough to get you through with your wheelchair.

- You can remove the door altogether and hang a full-length curtain in the doorway for privacy.

- You can also cut out the door-jamb molding from the floor to a height of about three feet. This will allow a bit more clearance to get your wheelchair through the door.

If thresholds pose a problem for you, take them out. Or replace the steep threshold with a broader one that is beveled on both sides, and forms a miniature ramp (as illustrated here).

DOOR CLOSERS

Another time you may encounter problems if you use a walker, wheelchair, or cane is when closing a door behind you. One simple solution is to tie a length of cord or ribbon around the doorknob, making a long loop, as illustrated on p. 69. Grab the ribbon loop as you enter the doorway, hold it as you go through, and then simply pull the door closed behind you.

Here is another simple door closer you can make.

You will need:

3 screw eyes

6' of Venetian-blind cord (or other strong, smooth cord)

1 easily grasped ring-shaped handle (as shown in the illustration). The handle should be heavy enough to keep the cord hanging straight.

Directions:

1. Screw one screw eye into the top corner of the door, and another screw eye into the top of the door frame, making sure the screw eye is not in the way of the door when it's closed. The third screw eye goes into the face of the door molding, at a point slightly higher than the doorknob.

2. Tie the cord to the screw eye in the top corner of the door and run the cord through the second and third screw eyes. Tie the handle to the end of

the cord, and let the cord hang next to the door.

By grasping the handle and pulling the cord, you can easily close the door behind you.

You can make closers for doors throughout your home using this method. You will have to figure out where the screw eyes need to be so that the cord pulls in the right direction.

MAKING SLIDING GLASS DOORS EASIER TO USE

If you use a wheelchair, walker, or cane, you may have a problem getting over the high threshold of your sliding glass doors. You may also have a problem opening a sliding glass door, because of the force needed to move the sliding glass panel away from the tight weather seal. Some solutions to these problems have been developed at the Center for Accessible Housing at North Carolina State University.

- To modify high thresholds and deep sliding door tracks, install wooden "mini-ramps" on both sides of the threshold (as shown). The new threshold you create should have a gradual slope of 1" rise over a 12" width on each side of the door.

- Attach appliqués or decals to your sliding glass doors so you can see whether they are open or closed.

- To allow sliding glass doors to slide more easily, remove the factory-installed weather stripping on both vertical sides of the receiving channel on the locking jamb (as shown in the picture). Replace that factory seal with a compressible, adhesive-backed foam weather-stripping on the back edge of the receiving channel. This will create a weather-tight seal that doesn't grip the door, and will make the door much easier to slide open or closed.

LEVER DOOR HANDLES

You can buy different types of lever door handles ready-made, and you can also buy lever door-handle adapters to slip over regular doorknobs. Consider this inexpensive, durable homemade alternative, however.* It works very well, doesn't get in the way of doorknob locking mechanisms, and costs very little.

You will need:

1 4" or 6" pipe-hanger bracket (available at plumbing supply stores)
1 2" diameter radiator hose clamp
plastic tape

Directions:

1. Using a pair of pliers, bend the two prongs of the pipe-hanger bracket so they are curved to match the curve of the doorknob (as shown).

2. Fit the radiator hose clamp and the pipe-hanger bracket onto the doorknob. Leave the screw a bit loose so you can adjust the position of the pipe-hanger bracket.

3. Make sure the bracket is in a comfortable position for you to use as a lever. And make sure the tightening screw is positioned so that it won't be in the way.

4. Tighten the screw securely to fasten the pipe-hanger bracket to the doorknob.

5. Because the radiator hose clamp has rough edges and the prongs of the pipe-hanger bracket are sharp, wrap the clamp and prongs with plastic or electrical tape.

6. Your new lever door handle can be wrapped with colored plastic tape to match your decor.

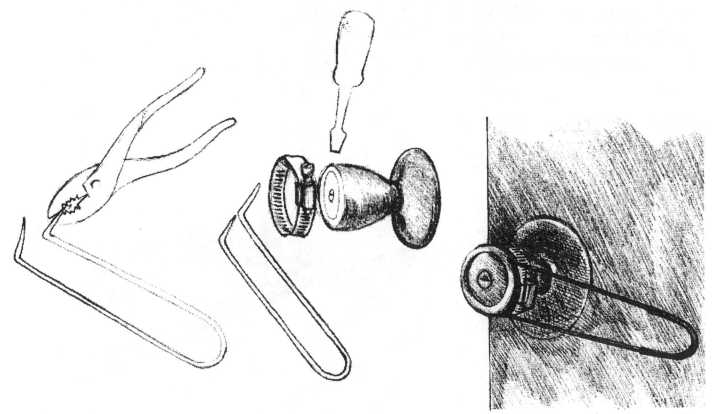

* Thanks to Therese Willkomm for this idea.

STAIR MODIFICATIONS

Stairs can pose a danger, particularly to older people. Falling on stairs is one of the most frequent causes of injury, second only to falls in bathrooms. Some simple precautions will make your stairs safer.

- Handrails should always be installed on both sides of a stairway, if possible. You can even add a third handrail up the middle of the staircase, if it's a wide one. Handrails should start before the bottom step and end beyond the top step, so you can get a firm grasp at the top or bottom. Handrails should be round and installed approximately 1½" from the wall so you can get a good grasp. They should be sturdy enough to support a minimum of 250 pounds at any point.

- Lighting in the stairway is very important, but you should avoid glare. Lights should illuminate the top and bottom of the staircase, as well as its full run. An easily reachable light switch at the top and bottom of the stairs makes it convenient to turn on the lights whether going up or down. Switches should be located at least one full stride (36") away from the first step so you will not step onto the stairs in darkness.

- Stairs must not be slippery, and if the stairs are carpeted, the carpets should not be loose or have protruding tacks or edges.

- If you use a walker or cane, and there is enough room, you can broaden stairs so that each step is deep enough for you to stand on comfortably with your walker before you climb to the next one. A suggested depth is at least 24". The height of steps can also be decreased, with more, broader steps replacing the old ones. Install handrails that match the dimensions of the new steps.

- A strip of white paint at the edges of steps makes them easier to see at night. Avoid deep pile carpeting on steps. You can carpet the steps themselves in one pattern and the floor at the bottom of the steps another pattern to help distinguish them—for example, you could use a tweed pattern on the floor and a solid or muted stripe pattern on the steps.

- The projection of a tread over a riser is called the "nosing." Nosings should project as little as possible (no more than 1") because they can be a tripping hazard. Carpeting a stairway can eliminate a nosing problem. Alternatively, you can bevel or round the underside edge of the nosing or add trim or molding strips on the riser.

LIGHT SWITCH EXTENSION

If you are using a wheelchair, or if you can't reach your arm up, it may be difficult for you to use a wall-mounted light switch. An extension handle is a very simple solution to the problem of a wall switch that's too high. This project takes only a few minutes.

Directions:

1. Drill a small (5/64 or 3/32") hole through the end of your light switch (as shown). This is easier to do if the switch plate is removed, but it can be done with the switch plate in place, because the hole does not have to be exactly straight across. It's a good idea to turn off the breaker or fuse first.

2. Drill a similar hole through the end of a piece of 3/8" dowel (as shown). The length of the dowel depends on your reach, but keep in mind that if the dowel is too heavy, the light switch may not stay in the "up" position.

3. Loosely attach the dowel to the light switch by twisting thin wire into a loop. Tuck the ends of the wire in.

4. Paint the dowel to match the wall to make it less visible, or, if you need to make the handle more visible, paint it a contrasting color.

5. A small, lightweight ball or ornament can be fastened to the bottom of the dowel stick for easier grasping, but again, remember that if the handle is too heavy, the light switch may not stay in the "up" position.

A light switch with a "positive action"—one that "snaps" into the up and down positions—works better than a silent/mercury switch.

A lightweight acrylic plastic rod can be used instead of a dowel, but may be more difficult to drill.

HOUSEHOLD WIRING

If you are thinking of upgrading your household electrical system, now may be the time to make it accessible and adaptable. Here are some suggestions taken from *Building for a Lifetime* (see the Resources section for more information about this excellent book) that may help to guide you.

- A surface-mounted cable raceway permits new wiring to be added easily and simply. Label the cables to keep track of them.

- Place new outlets higher than usual: 30" to 44" from the floor is suggested. Although many homes seem to have enough outlets, many of the outlets are inaccessible because they are obstructed by furniture.

- Locate light switches at all room entrances on the side nearest the door handle. Switch placement throughout the house should be at a consistent height and distance from the door frame. A height of 40" to 44" above the floor is best.

- At least one light in each room should be controlled by the wall switch, because permanently installed wall switches are easier to manipulate than the switches on most lamps.

- Locate three-way switches carefully (in sight of the room or stairway) so that one person can't inadvertently turn off the wrong light, putting another person into darkness.

- Avoid light switches that require a high degree of finger dexterity. Use rocker or paddle switches. Light switches with internal lights are easily located in the dark.

- Install ground-fault-interrupted outlets (GFIs). These devices shut the current off if you come in contact with a "hot" wire. GFIs are lifesavers and well worth installing.

- Appliances that are out of reach (for example, an air conditioner or kitchen range hood) can be adapted by leaving the appliance on and plugging the unit into an outlet controlled by a wall switch.

WALKER ACCESSORIES

If you use a walker to help you get around, both of your hands are occupied, and carrying small items from place to place can be a problem. Here are a couple of ideas that were developed by people who use walkers.

Bicycle Bottle*

To keep a supply of cold water nearby throughout the day, fill a bicycle bottle one-third of the way full with water and put the bottle in the freezer the night before. In the morning, fill the bottle with cold water. The melting ice will keep the water cold all day.

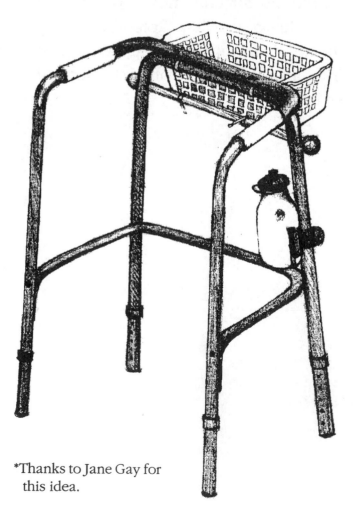

*Thanks to Jane Gay for this idea.

Bicycle bottles come with brackets that can be easily attached to the frame of your walker. If the bracket is too large, pad it with some hot-water-pipe insulation.

Hanging Basket/Tote Bag/Tray

There are many types of useful, inexpensive baskets, trays, and totes. But it may be tricky to attach one of these containers to your walker so that it doesn't swing and is strong enough to safely carry your belongings. This design solves both those problems.

You will need:
1 container or basket of your choice
1 ½" dowel about 18" long
2 1¼" diameter round wooden "head beads" (with ½" holes) from a craft shop
tie-wrap fasteners

Directions:

1. Select a container the right shape for you. Remember that if it's too deep, you may have trouble reaching the bottom. Use two plastic tie-wraps to fasten the container to the top frame of the walker, as shown.

2. About 1" up from the base of the container, measure the distance across the walker, from outer edge to outer edge of the aluminum tubing. Add ½" and cut the dowel to this length.

3. Use two tie-wraps to attach the dowel to the container as shown. Glue one "head bead" on each end of the dowel to keep it from shifting. Trim the ends of the tie-wraps, making sure the edges cannot scratch you.

Simple Walker Bag

The walker bag is a convenient, washable, two-pocket carry-all that attaches to a walker and can hold paperback books, eyeglasses, tissues, medicines, and other lightweight items. This is a simple sewing project and makes a nice gift. No cutting is needed, just some simple sewing.

You will need:

1 hand or dish towel, approximately 15" x 24"

safety pins or sew-on Velcro tape fastener

sewing thread

Directions:

1. Fold the towel in half (as illustrated) with the decorated sides together, and then fold back one side so the hemmed edge lines up with the halfway fold. The decorated side will be showing now. The double-folded part will form the pockets.

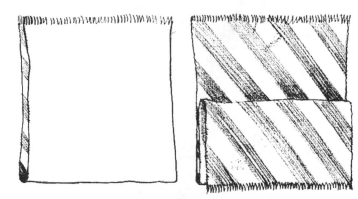

2. Pin the edges of the pockets and sew all three layers of fabric along the two edges of the bag. Reinforce your stitching at the top of the pocket.

3. Sew another line of stitching down the middle as shown in the drawing, dividing the pocket into two equal sections.

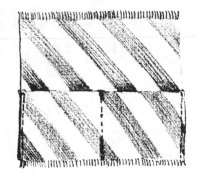

Reinforce your stitching at the top of the middle seam. The seams form two pockets.

5. The bag can be easily fastened to the walker with safety pins as shown, or with strips of sew-on Velcro tape; or you can sew on buttons and make button-

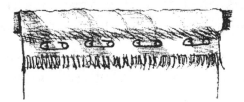

holes to fasten it to the walker. Safety pins are the easiest, and they make the bag easily removable for washing.

A variation on this idea is to make a narrow, deep bag out of terrycloth, to carry a cordless telephone, knitting needles, or a rolled-up magazine.

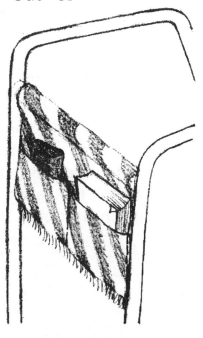

USING LONG HANDLES TO EXTEND YOUR REACH

If it's difficult for you to bend down or reach up high, it may be helpful to put a long handle on an everyday item. Unfortunately, just extending a handle can make matters worse, because when you add a long handle to a heavy object, you are adding weight and changing the balance. So make sure, if you are extending the handle on a tool, or if you are using a broom or other long-handled tool, that you use lightweight materials.

This project shows how to add a light-weight extension handle to a feather duster, but you can use the same idea to extend the handles of many other household objects.

You will need:

1 lightweight feather duster
1 ¼ or ⅜" dowel, 1 to 2 feet long
tie-wraps or plastic tape
foam hot-water-pipe insulation
plastic tape to wrap around the insulation

Directions:

1. Put the pieces together as shown in the picture.

2. Use tie-wraps or tape to fasten the object to the handle. Slip a piece of foam hot-water-pipe insulation onto the end of the handle and wrap plastic tape snugly around it.

As you can see, there are three important parts:

a. a lightweight object
b. a lightweight extension handle
c. a lightweight built-up hand grip

Remember, the handle itself does not have to be thick and heavy as long as you build up the hand grip to a comfortable size for your hand.

Other lightweight solutions:

- A small, angled mirror at the end of a lightweight, long handle is wonderful for searching "high and low" for something.

- Drop a button or a pin? A piece of double-sided carpet tape or a loop of scotch cellophane tape (sticky side out) on the end of a dowel is great for picking small objects off the floor.

ONE-HANDED BROOM

This project makes a broom comfortable and effective for use with one hand. It works equally well with a leaf rake, a garden hoe, or any other similar tool. Because it is designed for your individual measurements, try it with an old discarded broomstick first, so you can make size adjustments if necessary.

You will need:

1 broom or mop to be modified
1 radiator hose clamp approximately 1" in diameter
1 roundhead screw approximately 1" long
2 flathead screws approximately ³/₄" long
(Use whatever size screws and hose clamp you have available.)
1 empty, large, plastic liquid laundry detergent jug
moleskin for padding (optional)

Directions:

1. To make the wooden hand grip, cut 5" off the end of the broom handle.

2. Open the radiator hose clamp and enlarge one of its slits by forcing a nail through it into a block of scrap wood.

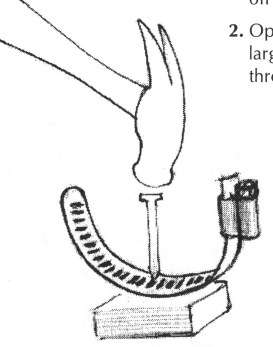

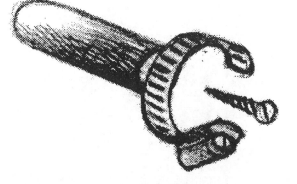

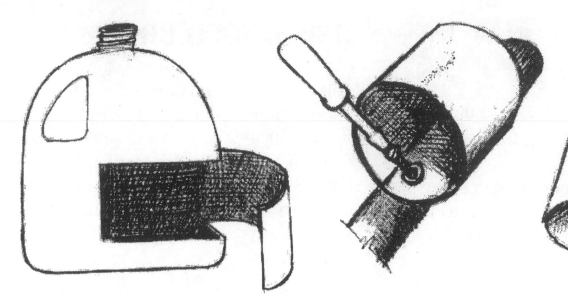

3. Make a small pilot hole in the sawed end of the 5" piece of broomstick and securely screw the roundhead screw through the clamp into the pilot hole.

4. Attach the assembled handle to the broomstick as shown.

5. Cut a smooth 3" x 12" strip of plastic from the detergent jug. Turn it inside out (the plastic is easier to work with inside out). Heat a nail or small screwdriver and pierce the cylinder in two places as shown.

6. Make two corresponding small pilot holes in the broomstick and use the flathead screws to fasten the plastic to the broomstick.

7. Cover the screw heads and the edge of the plastic with moleskin, if desired.

HAVE YOU THOUGHT ABOUT THIS?

Housekeeping

Organization is the key to accomplishing the tasks you *can* do yourself; delegation (to other people) is the key to accomplishing the tasks that you *can't* (or shouldn't) do yourself.

- **Equipment**: Use small, lightweight brooms and mops. An ordinary broom is a heavy weight attached to the end of a long lever, and can impose increased stress on your arms. "Convenience" appliances are not always designed with convenience in mind. Their buttons and knobs may be too small; the device may be too heavy. Try it before you buy it.

- **Laundry**: If you use a wheelchair and have a top-loading washing machine, hang a securely anchored angled mirror so you can see down into the washer (see the recommendation for the kitchen stove area on p. 40). Organize your laundry area so you can sit down, and so that you have adequate work space at a height that is best for you. To avoid bending, use a reacher to get garments out of the washing machine or dryer. (See the Resources section for specialty catalogs.) Adapt the knobs on your washer or dryer, or use a purchased knob turner.

- **Ironing**: Sit down while you're ironing, and use a lightweight plastic iron or travel iron. It should turn itself off automatically if you forget to. Stop doing nonessential ironing.

- **Cleaning**: Keep duplicate sets of cleaning supplies on each floor of your home. Use a four-wheeled utility cart to carry your supplies from one room to another. Support your mop bucket on a small wheeled dolly (round plastic dollies are commonly sold for use under large flower pots). While you're doing chores around the house, rest frequently, and protect your skin and lungs from household chemicals.

- **Vacuuming**: If you drop the wand of your canister vacuum cleaner and can't bend down to pick it up, straighten out an old wire coat hanger and use the hanger's hook (unbent a little bit) to retrieve the fallen vacuum cleaner wand. Leave heavy vacuuming to others, or use a lightweight electric broom yourself.

- **Bedmaking**: Cut open one corner of your fitted sheet and attach tabs of Velcro fastener tape to reclose it. That way you don't have to lift the corner of the mattress when you change sheets. Switch to lighter, knitted sheets. Use lightweight blankets and comforters. Make half of the bed at a time.

Getting Around

- Wherever you need to go around the house, you should have a clear 36"-wide pathway with no abrupt changes in floor level. Rearrange your traffic pattern to achieve this. Move clutter out of the way.

- Install grab bars and handrails wherever you might need them; grab bars are not just for bathrooms, and handrails are not just for stairways. Put corner guards on sharp corners of furniture that you might bump or fall against.

- Doors can be difficult to open and shut, particularly if you use a walker, wheelchair, or cane. Remove a bothersome door and install a full-length curtain with large curtain rings, so the curtain can slide easily.

- Wall-to-wall carpeting should be low-pile. Remember that carpeting retains dust that might aggravate any respiratory problems you have. A thick carpet can also be a problem when you use a wheelchair to get around. Even low-pile carpeting increases the effort it takes to propel a wheelchair.

- Throw rugs are dangerous, but if you must have them, make sure they have nonslip backings. Remember that nonslip backing and double-sided carpet tape age and lose their effectiveness. Check the backs of your throw rugs periodically.

- On floors, glare can be visually confusing. Avoid high-glare floor wax or high-gloss vinyl floor covering. If you have hardwood floors, make sure you use nonslip wax.

- Wall outlets may need to be a little higher and light switches a little lower than standard height. Make sure that both are easily accessible.

- If you use a walker, you know how hard it is to carry things. Try wearing a "fanny pack"—a zipped purse that is worn around your waist.

- Use color and paint as visual cues. Paint your doors or door frames in a contrasting color so you can see them more easily. Paint a bright (preferably white) strip of paint on the edge of each stair step. Install switch plates that contrast with the color of the wall, so they are easier to find.

- Train your pets to stay away from your feet when you are walking. Try to keep their toys away from pathways in your house.

- If your wheelchair or walker makes scuff and scrape marks on the wall, protect heavy wear areas on the wall with Plexiglas sheets, drilled and screwed to the wall. Or use carpet sample squares (usually available cheaply at a carpet store) attached to the wall with tacks, glue, or double-sided tape.

SOME COMMERCIALLY AVAILABLE PRODUCTS

Housekeeping

Numerous commercially available items can help make your housekeeping work easier. Again, shop around before you purchase—there are lots of choices.

- **Mesh bags** make laundry easier to handle. When placed in these bags, fragile garments can be washed in a washing machine instead of by hand. You can also place several small items together in a bag to make them easier to retrieve from the washing machine.

- **Aerosol can adapters** fit a wide variety of aerosol containers and change the hand movement needed for aerosol activation from pushing a button to gently squeezing a handle.

- **Long-handled dust brushes and pans** make it possible to pick up dirt without having to bend over. Likewise, a long-handled tub brush is perfect for scrubbing your bathtub.

- **Furniture glides** are available from many catalogs. Slip them underneath a heavy piece of furniture, and it will move easily for cleaning.

Getting Around

Many commercially available devices can help you get around. Because there are so many styles and models, look in several specialty catalogs before you make a decision.

- **Sliding transfer boards** can be placed between your wheelchair and your bed, chair, or commode. Then, with or without help, you slide along the board to transfer from one place to another.

- Many styles of **lap trays and carryall bags** can be attached to wheelchairs. If you look through several catalogs you will find a type that suits you.

- **Cane clips** are available for clipping your cane to a table edge, to your walker or wheelchair, or to a wall. Other cane "accessories" include a clip-on flashlight and a portable clip-on alarm that emits a loud signal when you press a button.

- **Reachers** are aids that you use to get items below or above your reach (instead of bending or reaching). They come in many sizes and shapes. The most common reachers are a length of rod with a pair of jaws on one end, and a trigger grip on the other end. Medium-length ones (around 30" long) seem to be the favorites for picking things up from the floor and reaching up high.

CAREGIVER NOTES

All too often older people become disabled *by* their environment—becoming, in effect, prisoners in a home full of obstacles and barriers. Visualize a narrow doorway into a bathroom and a person in a wheelchair sitting outside the door, unable to get through the doorway. If you ask yourself, "What is the problem? Why can't this person get into the bathroom?" your first answer will likely be, "Because the person is in a wheelchair." But think again. The problem is not with the person. The better answer is, "Because the doorway is too narrow."

- Look around the house. Ask the older person to think about tasks that are difficult, and brainstorm together about solutions. Many obstacles can be removed by making simple changes, but decisions should come about by working together. It's a matter of self-respect and independence. Think about how you would feel having someone come into your home and change things around for "your own good." So don't make the changes on your own. A partnership is best, although suggestions can come from either party. This chapter is a good place to start in your problem-solving process.

- Environmental barriers can be hazardous as well as limiting. Very gradual changes associated with aging can make a friendly home increasingly hazardous for an older person. And because there is no clear point in time when an older person will realize a task is risky, your attention, as caregiver, to safety and injury prevention is vitally important. We cannot solve every problem, but we can make many modifications in the environment that will allow an older person to have more independence in a safer home environment.

- It would be impossible to write sensibly and comprehensively about safety on a single page, but because there is such a high rate of accidental injury among older people, a lot of reference material is readily available. For an excellent source of information, we recommend sending for a free copy of:

Safety for Older Consumers
Home Safety Checklist
U.S. Consumer Product Safety Commission
Washington, DC 20207

CHAPTER

Outdoor Activities & Home Security

PORCHES AND PATIOS

Sitting on a front porch talking to neighbors, or resting on a patio in the shade of an umbrella—everybody enjoys an outdoor area that is comfortable to use. If you are lucky enough to have a porch or patio, or are planning to build one, keep these ideas in mind.

- Extend the usable season of a porch or patio by adding a Plexiglas windscreen that lets the warm sunlight through but blocks the wind. The porch or patio can be L-shaped and fit around the corner of your house so that both sun and shade can be enjoyed. The porch can be protected from the weather by a roof or awning. A large umbrella at a patio table can provide shade. There are also shade umbrellas that can be clamped onto a wheelchair.

- Night lighting should be bright enough to see steps and obstacles. Install a lighted doorbell. Clearly mark the edge of each step with a stripe of bright paint.

- Make sure the railing around the porch or patio is sturdy. Install railings on both sides of the steps, and if the porch steps are wide, have a railing down the middle as well as on the sides, so that a person using the steps can comfortably grasp railings with both hands. For a person who uses a walker or cane, steps should have a shallow height and a width of at least 24" from front to back.

- Treated lumber can be very slippery; even a film of dew on your patio can be hazardous. (See our suggestions on pp. 87-88 for making wood less slippery underfoot.) Wood can also have rough edges. Keep banisters and railings smooth.

- To avoid having to stoop or bend, build or place a shelf or small table next to the entranceway so you can place your packages on it while unlocking and opening the door.

- A ramp can be built right into a deck or porch. A gentle 1:20 rise (see p. 87) can lead to an acces-

sible porch that goes right up to the door sill without any steps.

- Porch furniture must be sturdy. Lightweight chairs can overturn easily. To modify a picnic table for wheelchair use, extend one end of the tabletop by bolting on a rectangle of exterior-grade plywood.

RAMPS

Every household's ramp requirement is unique. The shape and layout of the house, the lay of the land, the location of the driveway, and the person who will be using the ramp all make a difference. You might combine the new ramp with a deck or patio as an outdoor recreation area for the whole family. Put the ramp at the rear door if it is closer to ground level than the front door. Or take out a window and put in an entirely new door for your ramped entrance.

- Ramps must not be steeper than 1:12, meaning that a ramp rises 1" for every 12" in length. Wheelchair users prefer 1:20, 1" rise for every 20" of length — or as close to this ratio as you can get in the space you have. If the wheelchair will always be pushed up and down by an assistant, 1:12 is acceptable. If you have a helper, make sure that you go down the ramp backward so that the chair doesn't roll away.

- If you live in an area where the ground freezes in the winter, footers supporting the ramp must be set well below the frost line. Snow and ice can make a ramp unusable. Partially protect a ramp from snow by extending your roof so that the ramp is covered. Storm-window plastic stapled along the outer railing can help prevent snow from drifting onto the ramp. Wheelchairs can track snow and mud into the house, so include a mud-room or vestibule at the entrance for wheelchair cleaning. Or install a plastic carpet runner inside the doorway to protect your carpet.

- Most people use lumber to build ramps. As with any other outdoor project, treated lumber is recommended. Plywood should be marine or exterior grade. Use twist nails or screws to assemble the ramp, and use galvanized nails that won't rust. Your local lumberyard or building company can help you with material selection. Build your ramp as solidly as you would build a deck.

- Traction on ramps is very important; wet, slippery ramps can be dangerous. Wood cleats are sometimes used on ramps when a helper will be pushing the wheelchair. Make sure that the strips are short enough that the wheelchair wheels straddle them. It is difficult to remove snow from ramps with cleats or cross strips.

  Most people improve traction by painting the ramp's surface with a mixture of fine sand and deck enamel. Fine sand can be purchased at your paint store and mixed into the paint using the paint shaker at the store. Or you can use regular sandbox sand. The coarser sandbox sand can be sprinkled liberally on the freshly painted surface a few inches at a time. The coarser the sand, the better the traction, but the faster it will wear off. During the winter, use a plastic snow shovel on a sand-painted ramp; a metal shovel tends to scrape off the sand.

  Instead of sand-paint, commercially

available, pressure-sensitive tape with a nonslip surface can be purchased. Don't use outdoor carpeting for ramp surfaces: moisture builds up and the wood rots underneath. If you are building a concrete ramp, make sure the surface is rough-troweled.

- Don't overlook the importance of safe and comfortable handrails. People using the ramp may rely on smooth, firmly anchored handrails on both sides of the ramp. If one of the handrails is attached to a wall, leave 2" between the rail and the wall for knuckle space. Average adults need handrails 32" above the surface of the ramp. Handrails can be made out of smoothly sanded 2" x 4" lumber, or out of 1¼" metal pipe. Handrail uprights should be spaced 36" apart and securely screwed or bolted into the ramp's base. The top ends of uprights should be cut at the same angle as the slope of the ramp. The handrail can be screwed to the sides or tops of the uprights.

- Curbs can be easily made from 2" x 4" lumber laid flat along the entire edge of the ramp and platform. These are a very important, but often overlooked, part of a ramp. Curbs are needed to prevent wheelchair wheels from slipping off the edge and to provide knuckle room between the large wheels and the railings.

- Safe lighting of the ramp and path must be a priority. Outdoor lighting doesn't have to be fancy, but it must be ad-equate. If possible, there should be light switches near the bottom of the ramp as well as at the doorway. An automatic outdoor lamp that uses a motion sensor can be included in your ramp planning.

- Doors should be at least 32" wide to accommodate a wheelchair comfortably. Doors should be lightweight, and doorknobs and handles (such as lever handles) should be matched to the person who will be using the ramp. The side on which the door is hinged is important. You can rehang an existing door if the direction of your ramp will prevent easy maneuvering in and out of the doorway.

  If you have a regular door that swings inward, and a storm door that swings outward, you will need a platform with enough room to make a safe, comfortable turn. Regulations require that the platform be 5' deep and extend 1' beyond each side of the door. Most people prefer a platform that is at least 6' square. The person using the ramp will want to approach an outward-swinging door on the latch side. If your entrance-way door swings in, the platform can be smaller (3' or 4' deep), and the person using the ramp will want to approach from the hinge side of the door. The platform width must extend at least one foot past each side of the door.

- Thresholds should not be higher than ½" to ¾". Beveling the threshold will make it easier to cross. Consider the space inside the entranceway as well as the space outside on the platform. Allow enough space to comfortably maneuver the wheelchair. A turning radius of at least 5' is required for a wheelchair.

- The legal minimum size of a ramp is very specific. Dimensions can be greater to suit your house and the way your ramp will be used. The minimum platform size depends on the way your door opens. Your ramp must be 36" wide, with a 60" level landing for every 30" of rise. If you plan to make an L-shaped or U-shaped ramp, there must be a landing at each turning point. At the bottom of the ramp, there must be a level pad — at least 6' of clear, flat space in which the person using the ramp can maneuver.

- House fires are a serious threat to all of us, and special considerations must be made if there is a person in your home who is physically unable to escape quickly and/or independently from a fire. Provide a special exit door and emergency ramp to get out of the house. Even if it must be steeper or less attractive than your primary ramp, build a secondary, emergency ramp directly from the ramp user's ground-floor bedroom, or from a back door. Make sure the interior area leading to the emergency ramp is wide enough, accessible, kept clear of clutter, and easily opened by the person who will need to use the ramp for a quick exit. Don't let snow block the emergency exit; keep the ramp shoveled. And, of course, have smoke detectors, with working batteries (test them regularly), located in the right places.

The Eastern Paralyzed Veterans Association has published an excellent brochure about fire emergency procedures for individuals with disabilities, *Wheeling to Fire Safety: Fire Emergency Procedures for Individuals with Disabilities* (see the Resources section).

SALT SHAKER FOR ICE MELTING

If you live in a cold climate and find it difficult to spread ice melter on your front steps or walk, this idea may be helpful. It can be made by a young person as a gift.

You will need:

1 small plastic laundry-detergent or fabric-softener jug with a screw-on top
drill with a ¼" bit
sandpaper or a sharp knife
snow-melting pellets

Directions:

1. Wash out the plastic jug very thoroughly.

2. Using a ¼" drill bit, drill several holes in the lid, as shown. This should be done by an adult, since the plastic tends to grab the drill bit. The holes should be drilled from the inside, with the top resting firmly on a large piece of scrap lumber. Burrs left by the drill bit can easily be removed with a sharp knife or sandpaper, as shown.

3. Pour about a cup of commercially available snow-melting pellets into the jug. Don't use plain rock salt — it cakes too easily and won't pour if it gets damp.

4. To use, turn the jug upside down, hold the handle, and shake the jug, sprinkling the snow remover wherever you need it.

5. You can decorate the shaker with contact paper or paint.

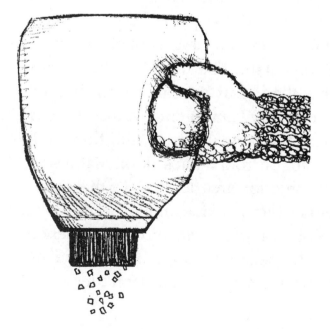

HANGING PLANT BASKET OR BIRD FEEDER

If you use a wheelchair, or if you have good strength in your arms but cannot reach high, a hanging plant basket or bird feeder may be just right for you. With a pulley system like the one illustrated, you can keep a hanging basket overhead, then lower it to tend the plant. Similarly, a bird feeder can be hung up under the eaves, safe from predators, and lowered to fill with birdseed.

CAUTION: Locate the screw eye and hook at least 3 feet from where the basket is hanging (as shown), so that if you lose control of the cord, the basket will not fall on you. Tie a knot in the rope so it will catch against a screw-eye and prevent the planter from falling more than a short distance.

You will need:

1 lightweight hanging plant or bird feeder
1 small pulley
1 screw-in hook
1 rope cleat
approximately 9' of nylon cord
2 screw eyes large enough to fit the cord through

Directions:

1. Firmly screw in the hook and screw eyes into a part of the porch structure that will support the weight. Hang the pulley from the hook.

2. Set the feeder or plant on a table under the pulley, on your wheelchair lap-tray, or wherever else you plan to work with it.

3. Run the cord up, through the pulley, and across to the first screw eye.

4. Tie a large knot in the cord just below the first screw eye. The knot should prevent the feeder or plant from falling lower than its position on the table or your lap-tray.

5. Run the cord down through the second screw eye and secure the cord to the rope cleat. The two screw eyes need to be at least as far apart as the vertical distance you expect to move the feeder or plant. Melt the loose end of the nylon cord to prevent unraveling.

PLANTER BOXES AND BENCH

If you enjoy gardening while you are sitting, and you are comfortable turning to the side, a combination planter box and bench may be an attractive addition to your patio. From dwarf fruit trees to carrots, you'll be amazed at what you can grow in a planter box with proper soil and sufficient light, water, and drainage.

Because we're concentrating on *your* comfort, we'll leave the plants' comfort to the gardening experts. Consult your local Cooperative Extension office, garden club, or other source of expert advice about plant varieties, sunlight, water, and proper potting mixture.

- For your comfort, the seating surface should probably be 18 to 19" off the floor or ground. This height will make it easier to get up and sit down, and to move from a wheelchair.

- Add simple D-shaped door handles on the top edges of the planter box to give you something to hold onto when you are getting up or sitting down, and for security while you are working.

- Make the planter boxes no larger than 24" x 24" so you can reach all the corners comfortably from your seat.

- Because the bench must be sturdy, you may need a professional carpenter to build the unit for you.

- Your local library will probably have many books of woodworking projects with building plans to select from. Many shapes and sizes of planter boxes are possible.

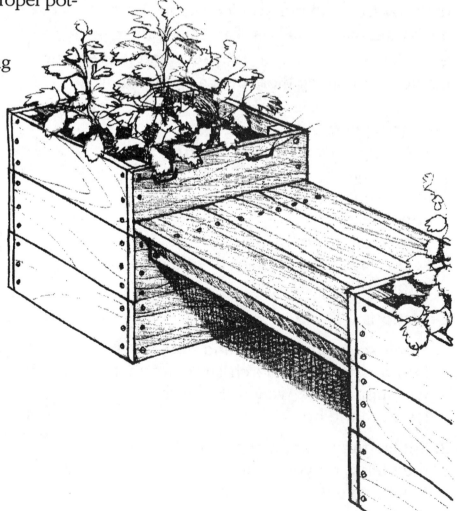

RAISED BEDS

If you will be gardening while standing, but have trouble bending over, a raised bed at comfortable working height may be just right for you. Raised beds are basically unmovable, bottomless boxes. They have vertical 4" x 4" supports that extend downward into the ground.

Raised beds can be made from naturally rot-resistant lumber such as redwood, railroad ties (select ones that haven't been treated with creosote), big wooden barrels, brick, or stonework. Even tires stacked up and bolted together can be used. Be careful, though, about using treated lumber; find out which treatments are rated as safe for human contact.

An important advantage of gardening in raised beds is that you can construct a raised bed to suit your needs, whether you work in a standing or seated position. An important drawback is that if you are

seated, you will have to work sideways, which may not be very comfortable.

- Make sure the raised bed is small enough that you can reach all the corners. If you work from only one side, you probably don't want to make the bed wider than about 30". Double the width if you can work from both sides. Measure your reach by sitting parallel to a table (not with your legs underneath it) and measuring how far you can reach to the center of the table. And think carefully about whether you would be comfortable working in this position.

- Some experts feel that the best raised beds are thin-walled—made of 2" thick lumber rather than railroad ties—in part because railroad ties are more difficult to fasten together. You will have to reinforce thin-walled raised beds with a cable-and-turnbuckle system across the center, because the weight of the soil will put a lot of outward pressure on the bed's walls.

- Raised beds need less watering than containers because of their larger soil volume. Use gardening labor-saving tricks. Use mulch as much as you can. Set up a watering system so you don't have to carry water to the plants. Arrange a convenient place to store your tools nearby. Provide a shady rest place for yourself.

- Remember, you can get lots of gardening advice from your Cooperative Extension office or local nursery.

SMALL GARDEN TOOLS

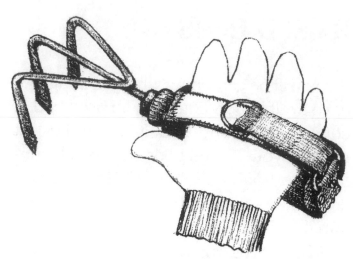

If you have arthritis in your hands, try padding the handles of your garden tools with foam hot-water-pipe insulation and wrapping the handles with plastic tape (see p. 9 for a similar adaptation for a hairbrush). If you have little or no finger strength, try this modification for the handle of your trowel or other small garden tool. Use Velcro tape fastener to adjust the tightness of the grip support, but make sure you don't make the strap so tight that circulation to your fingers is decreased. All these supplies (except for screws and pipe insulation) are available where sewing notions are sold.

You will need:

2   1-inch D-rings
14" of 1¼"-wide cotton webbing tape
3" of 1"-wide sew-on Velcro, **loop** side
2" of 1"-wide sew-on Velcro, **hook** side
4   #6 x ½" flat- or roundhead wood screws
5" of ¾" hot-water-pipe insulation

Directions:

1. Cut a 3" piece of webbing. Fold it in half with the D-ring in the middle. Drill two pilot holes in the end of the trowel handle and attach the webbing and D-ring as shown, using two screws.

2. Sew the pieces of Velcro tape fastener and D-ring to the 11" piece of webbing as shown in the picture.

3. Drill two pilot holes in the top of the handle as shown. Be- c a u s e the inner shank is metal, you cannot drill toward the center of the handle.

4. Attach the webbing (Velcro hook side down) to the handle using two screws. Make sure the screws are following the downward path of the pilot hole.

5. Pass the D-ring on the long strap through the other D-ring on the end of the handle (turn the D-ring sideways to make it fit through).

To use the trowel, place your weak hand on the trowel handle in a normal position. Holding onto the D-ring with your strong hand, tighten the Velcro strap so your weak hand is held snugly. Padding with the foam insulation is suggested. If you use the tool without padding, wear a gardening glove or cover the screw heads with tape to avoid abrasions on your palm.

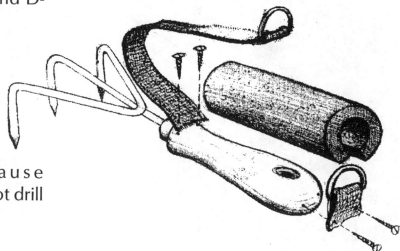

GARDENING WITH ONE HAND

There are easy ways to fix two-handed garden tools so they'll be comfortable to use with one hand. The idea is to stabilize the handle so it doesn't wobble when you are only holding on with one hand.

In Chapter 5, we converted a broom for use with one hand (see pp. 79-80). Here is another way of converting a long-handled tool. You can fix up a hoe or a leaf rake this way (or a broom if you want to).

Directions:

1. Take a forearm crutch and remove the bottom part of the crutch by releasing the pins that hold it in place. **Note:** Discarded forearm crutches are often available at local hospitals, physical therapists' offices, or medical equipment loan closets. You can also ask at your local Office for the Aging.

2. The best length for your one-handed hoe depends on how tall you are, how long your arm is, and whether you are going to use it while standing or while sitting in a wheelchair.

3. To "custom fit" this modification, we suggest that you and a helper loosely tape or rubber-band the hoe and crutch together, as illustrated here. Position the crutch/hoe on your arm and reach your arm forward. Adjust the length of the crutch/hoe so that the head of the hoe touches the ground at a comfortable distance in front of you.

4. Mark the right length on the hoe handle. Cut off the hoe handle about 3" higher than the mark so it can be inserted into the bottom portion of the crutch.

5. In order to insert the wooden hoe handle, you may have to taper it a bit by sanding or whittling it. Secure the crutch to the hoe handle by screwing roundhead screws through the crutch's original pin openings and into the hoe handle.

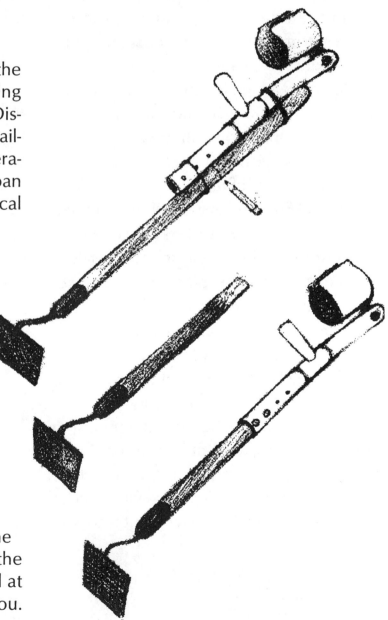

CONTAINER GARDENING

Perhaps a raised bed is the idea that comes to mind most frequently when people think of accessible gardening. But other alternatives may be more comfortable for you. Container gardens are not something you have to settle for—they are a passion in themselves. Look in your library or bookstore for detailed how-to books on container gardens.

What kinds of containers should you use for plants? Drainage is probably most important from the plants' point of view, but your comfort should be the most important consideration. Containers can include everything from a big old farm wagon, planted with magnificent tulip bulbs, to an old pair of leather work boots, filled with soil and lush green foliage that drapes over the sides. Whatever kind of containers you decide to use, make sure they are small enough that you don't have to reach too far. You should be able to work in a comfortable position.

Containers can be placed for easy access from a variety of positions. Containers can sit on wheeled dollies or carts that you can move in and out of shelter and sunlight. A wheelbarrow or a child's wagon can hold and move containers easily.

Start small. It can be very frustrating to undertake a project that is too ambitious for your strength. And don't forget that with light from a window, or with special electric lights, you can grow plants indoors as well.

HOMEMADE SEED TAPE

There are several things you can do to make planting seeds easier. Mix tiny seeds with sand or parakeet gravel, or even with dry used coffee grounds. Then put the seed/sand mixture into an empty shaker container. (Save a container from a dried spice or herb.) Or sow the mixture directly into the garden. Using light-colored sand or parakeet gravel to mix with the seeds will help you see where you've already sprinkled them. Cover the seeds with fine soil or sand as usual.

Another wonderful hint is to make your own seed tapes — invented by a creative gardener and written up in *Accessible Gardening for People with Physical Disabilities* (look for this book in the Resources section). This would make a wonderful winter project to do with a grandchild. You can mark the spots on the newspaper strips, and your helper can apply the paste and the seeds.

Directions:

1. Cut newspaper strips about 1" wide. (If you cut strips off the edge of a newspaper page, you can make sure the strips are straight.)

2. Mix a sticky paste of flour and water — the consistency of thick gravy or soft

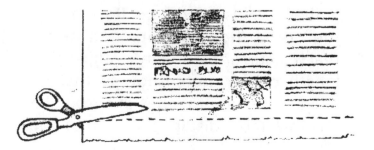

pudding seems to work well.

3. Using a Q-tip or small artist's paintbrush as an applicator, dab paste on the newspaper strip, spacing the dabs the right distance apart for the type of seed you're planting.

4. Place a seed on each dab and set the strip aside to dry. Both large and small

seeds lend themselves to this method, but you may find that tweezers are helpful in handling smaller seeds.

5. Plant the seed tapes in a furrow, seed side up, and cover as you normally would.

6. Keep seeds and seedlings well watered.

HOUSEHOLD SECURITY

Doors

You should feel secure and safe in your home. You should be able to get in easily, and out quickly in an emergency. Here are some considerations to think about.

- Locks are often installed too high for an older person to use comfortably. Don't install any door hardware higher than 48" above the floor — 40" to 44" is even better, especially for a person using a wheelchair.

- Sliding glass doors often have locks at both the top and the bottom. These can be difficult to operate. If you are shopping for one of these doors, look for one with a large latch you can operate with your closed fist.

- Use locks and bolts that you can operate. If you can't see a keyhole or manipulate a lock, make changes. Although you can use a slide-bolt instead of a deadbolt, it's much better to use a deadbolt with a "panic release" that is operated by an inside lever doorhandle.

- Holding, inserting, and turning a key can be very difficult. Keyless lock sets use a numbered keypad that you activate by punching in a combination of numbers. Some of these lock sets have very small buttons, so make sure you can see and handle the lock before you have it installed.

- Have a peephole in your exterior door. If you use a wheelchair, or if the existing peephole is too high, add another one at a better height. To measure, touch your nose to the door at your usual height (using your walker, your cane, or your wheelchair.) The peephole should be located 1½" higher than your "nose height." Because a peephole has a wide-angle lens, even if it is installed at sitting height, you will be able to see the face of the person outside.

- There should be a good light outside your door so you can see the lock easily. Paint a white circle on the lock cylinder around where your key fits. Use white paint or waterproof typewriter correction fluid, and be careful not to fill the keyhole with it.

- If you use a wheelchair, make certain you have lots of maneuvering room at your exterior doorway. Don't forget to allow space to open the storm door.

- If you are shopping for a door, remember that many glass door panels will be too high for a person sitting in a wheelchair to see out of.

Windows

Windows are important for psychological well-being and for security—from both the outside and the inside—so it is important that you can both see out of and operate the window. Most homes have vertical sliding sash windows. Often these windows bind and stick when you try to raise them. Sometimes they need to be raised and lowered using two hands. And sometimes they are too high to be reached by a person in a wheelchair.

- To open a wooden window more easily, put separate handles in the center of both the top and bottom rail of the sash. Begin opening the window by pushing up on the top rail, then continue by pushing up on the bottom rail.

- Every room should have an emergency door or window exit to the outside. Emergency escape windows are required to be at least 20" wide by 24" high, and have at least 5.7 square feet of openable area. This minimum size will probably not be enough if you have to be moved by someone else.

- If you are installing a new window, a sill height of 20" above the floor makes it a good emergency exit, and good for looking outside while lying in bed. If, however, the room will be used by children, a 20" sill height is too low for safety. A sill height of 30" is comfortable for looking outside from your armchair.

- If the locks on your windows are old, replace them. A window lock should be easy to operate and have a large lever. Make sure you can manipulate the lock in an emergency.

- Make sure you can operate any window security gates, chains, or locks. Ground-floor windows in older houses

KEY HOLDERS

and apartments may have metal accordion gates that are fastened with a hasp and padlock. These gates have often been in place for many years, and were difficult to open even when they were new. They provide security, but can be deadly in an emergency.

- Notify your fire department and put a safety sticker on your bedroom window if you will need help getting out of your bedroom in case of fire.

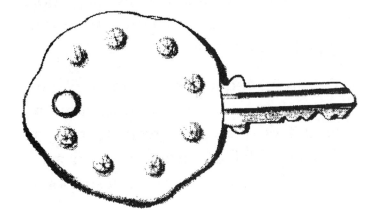

One of the most difficult movements you can make is to reach forward, grasp something, and turn your wrist, so it is no wonder that handling a house or car key can be hard. If you have difficulty grasping a key, try a homemade key holder. Key holders are made from materials easily purchased at a craft shop. You can really get artistic with this project. Make sure that you don't embed the key's shaft too deeply or you will interfere with its function.

If you have difficulty seeing the keyhole, use white paint (waterproof office correction fluid works well) to paint a little circle around the key hole. If you are making key holders for car keys, make sure the key will still fit into a recessed ignition switch.

Key Holder #1

A wonderful, colorful, modeling compound called **polymer clay** is available in craft stores. As easy to use as old-fashioned Plasticine modeling clay, this compound becomes hard and durable after being baked for a few minutes in a warm oven. Ask for Sculpey III™, Fimo™, or a similar compound at your local craft shop.

Make a simple key holder by patting two balls of compound into flat circles, and sandwiching the head of the key between them, squeezing gently to seal it. Make a hole for attachment to a keychain. After baking, the key holder can be painted with acrylic paint.

Key Holder #2

Another delightful craft material is "Friendly Plastic™," a sheet-plastic material that can be cut with scissors and then heat-softened and formed to shape. The material comes in many colors and patterns.

To make a key holder from this material, cut two small rectangles (approximately 1" x 3") with scissors. Following directions available at your craft shop, place one rectangle on a cookie sheet with the key positioned on it. Put the other rectangle on top of the first. Bake for about two minutes. The plastic pieces will melt together. A hole for a key chain can be drilled through the plastic when it is cool.

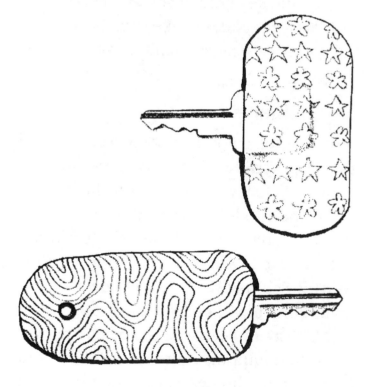

HAVE YOU THOUGHT ABOUT THIS?

Gardening

You can't handle a big garden any more? If you are one of those people who enjoy growing flowers or vegetables, nothing should stop you. Bring the planting level up to a more comfortable height with raised beds, or put soil into containers on a table-top. Gardening shouldn't have to stop being part of your life — summer or winter — if that's what you love.

Here are some ways to put gardening back into your life, or perhaps to discover gardening as a new hobby. You may not come across these hints in gardening books because they often pay more attention to plants than to people.

- Be careful about how you stake plants or mark rows. If you are unsteady on your feet, you don't want to take a chance of falling against a sharp garden stake. Plant cages or other supports are better.

- To keep your supplies nearby, create a storage place near your work area. Mount an old country mailbox on a post in your garden. You can store your small tools in it, and it's decorative as well.

- Don't overexert yourself. Put a seat near the garden so you can rest frequently. If you don't have a shady spot to sit, use a lawn umbrella for shade.

- Be aware of the sun: Avoid excessive sunlight, wear a protective hat, and apply sunscreen. If you have reduced skin sensitivity, be careful of possible scratches, abrasions, and skin breakdown.

- Be a problem solver. Think up your own ways to match planting, maintaining, and harvesting tasks to your abilities.

- Lightweight, child-size, or easy-to-grasp tools may be helpful. Try a flat box or tray on your lap for carrying things in your wheelchair. Attach a bicycle basket to your walker (see p. 76).

- Read one of the many books about gardening for people with physical limitations. Several of these how-to books are listed in the Resources section.

- Contact the Horticultural Therapy Association for more information. Their phone number is (800) 634-1603.

Feeling Secure

According to the National Crime Prevention Council's *Senior Citizens Against Crime*, "Although people over 65 are victims of crime far less frequently than young people, many senior citizens are so worried about crime that they shut themselves up in their homes and rarely go out. But isolating ourselves behind locked doors, not getting together with our neighbors, actually makes it easier for criminals to operate in the neighborhood."

Regardless of statistics, older people do feel afraid. You have the right to feel safe in your home, and some things can be done to increase your feeling of security.

- Lighting outside your home should be adequate to see clearly whatever is going on around the house. Install a light switch so you can control outside lights from the room you are most likely to be in at night—your bedroom.

- Work out a buddy system with a friend, and check on each other. Join (or start) a Neighborhood or Apartment Watch group.

- Ask the local crime prevention officer from your police or sheriff's office to come and talk to your senior-citizen group about security measures.

- Consider purchasing an emergency-button system that will activate an alarm to call for assistance. Information about these systems is available at your local Office for the Aging.

- Inquire about alarm systems, but make sure that you are able to see and manipulate the controls. Carefully evaluate your security requirements, your budget, and your physical abilities before you purchase an alarm system.

- If you feel that you would not be able to get out of your house quickly in case of emergency, contact your local fire department and tell them who you are and where you live.

• Get a telephone that can be programmed to automatically dial an emergency number if you punch a single button. The telephone should not be mounted on a wall, because if you fall, you may not be able to reach a wall phone.

CAREGIVER NOTES

Caregiving concerns don't stop at the front door. An older person should be able to maintain, as much as possible, his or her activities at home, in the backyard, and in the community.

Despite disability, an older person can often continue favorite activities like gardening. Despite failing health, an older person may enjoy watching the world from the front porch, or sitting in a warm sunny spot on the patio.

Unfortunately, while we can often adapt the interiors of our homes and apartments, the outdoors is another story. Sometimes the problem is an architectural or structural barrier; or it may be a landlord who does not want alterations to be made to the exterior of a dwelling. But many simple, often overlooked modifications can be made that will allow an older person to have greater freedom of movement outside the home.

Enhancing safety and security is another aspect of caregiving. As personal strength decreases, and as senses become less acute, the outside world can present new problems.

As caregivers, we worry about an older person's overconfidence and risk-taking behavior inside the home in a familiar setting. But we also worry about an older person's lack of confidence and insecurity when she or he ventures outside or into the community. Some older people become virtual prisoners in their own homes because of barriers, difficulties, or fear.

Home security is an issue that must be dealt with. An older person may view our concern as needless worrying, meddling, or even disrespect. Having always done things one way, he or she may see no reason to change habits now. So we have to expect some disagreements when we try to persuade an older person to make lifestyle changes for the sake of safety. There are no easy answers, but this chapter offers some of the structural solutions.

R E S O U R C E S

The Able Gardener: Overcoming Barriers of Age and Physical Limitations
by Kathleen Yeomans
ISBN 0-88266-789-0
1992 (298 pp.) $16.95
Garden Way Publishing
Storey Communications, Inc.
Schoolhouse Road
Pownal, VT 05261
A practical guide to gardening, including both gardening and disability information.

ABLEWARE
Maddak, Inc.
Pequannock, NJ 07440
(800) 443-4926 or (201) 628-7600
One of the most useful catalogs of adaptive equipment. You should also get the Enrichments catalog and the adaptAbility catalog, listed below, to compare prices.

Accent on Living Magazine
P.O. Box 700
Bloomington, IL 61702
Very useful quarterly publication "for people who happen to have a disability." Many answers to questions, practical tips, travel ideas, new products, etc. Subscription $10.00 per year.

Accessible Gardening for People with Physical Disabilities: A Guide to Methods, Tools and Plants
by Janeen R. Adil
ISBN 0-933149-56-5
1994 (300 pp.) $16.95
Woodbine House
6510 Bells Mill Rd.
Bethesda, MD 20817
(800) 843-7323
A great book about gardening—including what varieties of plants to grow, as well as the usual information about raised beds and adapted tools. Very specific, useful information for all ages of gardeners.

The Accessible Housing Design File
by Ronald L. Mace & Barrier-Free
    Environments
ISBN 0-442-00775-2
1991 (213 pp.) $44.95 plus $3.00 handling
Van Nostrand Reinhold
115 Fifth Avenue
New York, NY 10003
An invaluable resource for everyone involved with the design, construction, and management of housing for older and disabled individuals.

adaptAbility: Products for Rehabilitation & Therapy

P.O. Box 515
Colchester, CT 06415
(800) 266-8856

This catalog is one of the best. It includes many interesting adaptive aids as well as therapeutic devices and supplies. You should also get the *ABLEWARE* and *Enrichments* catalogs to compare prices.

American Association of Retired Persons (AARP)

601 E Street, N.W.
Washington, D.C. 20049
(800) 441-2277

National organization. Membership ($8.00) includes subscription to *Modern Maturity* magazine. Publishes free newsletter for health and aging professionals.

American Diabetes Association (ADA)

1660 Duke Street
Alexandria, VA 22314
(800) 232-3472

National organization with local affiliates who have local publications and support groups and can provide information.

American Foundation for the Blind (AFB)

15 West 16 Street
New York, NY 10011
(800) 232-5463

National organization to provide information. Free *Public Education Materials Catalogue* available.

American Heart Association

7272 Greenville Avenue
Dallas, TX 75231
(214) 373-6300

Numerous free brochures and booklets about many topics relevant to older people. Information about strokes, cardiovascular health, nutrition and cooking, etc.

The Arthritis Foundation

1314 Spring Street, N.W.
Atlanta, GA 30309
(800) 283-7800

National organization with chapters and clubs across the U.S. Membership is $20.00 and includes chapter newsletter and bi-monthly magazine, *Arthritis Today*. Numerous publications and videotapes available.

AT&T Special Needs Center

2001 Route 46
Parsippany, NJ 07054
(800) 233-1222

Special telephone-related equipment for people with visual and hearing impairments.

Building for a Lifetime: The Design and Construction of Fully Accessible Homes
by Margaret Wylde, Adrian Baron-Robbins and Sam Clark
ISBN 1-56158-036-8
1994 (295 pp.) $44.95
> *The Taunton Press*
> *63 S. Main Street / P.O. Box 5506*
> *Newtown, CT 06470*

Planning a new house or undertaking a small-scale remodeling project? This book will inspire you. Rich in valuable information on how to modify homes for accessibility, safety, and comfort.

Center for Accessible Housing Newsletter

> *North Carolina State University*
> *School of Design, Box 8613*
> *Raleigh, NC 27695*

Available in several formats including large print, Spanish, and audio cassette. The Center for Accessible Housing has several publications and a periodic newsletter. The Center is a valuable resource with well-thought-out ideas presented in very usable formats.

A Consumer's Guide to Home Adaptation

1989 (52 pp.) $9.50
> *The Adaptive Environments Center*
> *374 Congress Street, Suite 301*
> *Boston, MA 02210*
> *(617) 695-1225*

Brief book with checklists, lots of illustrations, and some practical descriptions of home modifications.

Courage Stroke Network

> *Courage Center*
> *3915 Golden Valley Road*
> *Golden Valley, MN 55422*
> *1-800-553-6321*

A network of over 800 stroke clubs and groups. Bimonthly newsletter "Stroke Connection" is available free. Information, books, videotapes, manuals.

Disabled Outdoors Magazine

> *HC80, Box 395*
> *Grand Marais, MN 55604*
> *(218) 387-9100*

A unique magazine for and by disabled sportspeople, with information and articles from all over the United States. Interested in accessible hunting, fishing, camping, scuba diving, or golf? Anything you want to know about outdoor sports is in this periodical.

The Do-Able, Renewable Home: Making Your Home Fit Your Needs

by John Salmen
1991 (36 pp.)
> *American Association of Retired Persons*
> *601 E Street, N.W.*
> *Washington, DC 20049*

A brief, but very informative book that may provide you with all the information you need, or at least will get you started in your search for resources.

Eighty-Eight Easy-to-Make Aids for Older People & for Special Needs
by Don Caston
ISBN 0-88179-019-2
$12.95 plus $1.50 handling
Hartley & Marks Publishers
P.O. Box 147
Point Roberts, WA 98281
Practical woodworking projects for the home with step-by-step instructions.

The Enabling Garden: Creating Barrier-Free Gardens
by Gene Rothert
1994 (150 pp.) $13.95
Taylor Publishing Company
1550 West Mockingbird Lane
Dallas, TX 75235
One of the best adaptive gardening books. Mr. Rothert, the president of the American Horticultural Therapy Association, is a wheelchair user. The book is comprehensive, inspirational, and very positive.

Enrichments: **Products to Enhance Your Life**
P.O. Box 471
Western Springs, IL 60558
(800) 323-5547
Very useful catalog of adaptive equipment for a wide range of needs. The catalog is the consumer version of the Fred Sammon catalog written for rehabilitation and healthcare professionals.

The Gadget Book
edited by Dennis R. LaBuda for the
American Society on Aging
ISBN 0-673-24819-4
1985 (156 pp.)
American Association of Retired Persons (AARP)
601 E Street, N.W.
Washington, DC 20049
(800) 441-2277
A wonderful book with 350 commercially available products and ingenious devices for easier living. This compilation is clearly illustrated and useful.

Guide to Independent Living for People with Arthritis
by the Arthritis Health Professions Association
ISBN 0-912423-03-X
1988 (415 pp.)
Arthritis Foundation
1314 Spring Street, N.W.
Atlanta, GA 30309
A wonderful, down-to-earth book with thousands of suggestions, products, and strategies. Useful not only for people with arthritis, but for anyone who has problems with everyday tasks.

Homes that Help: Advice from Caregivers for Creating A Supportive Home for People with Alzheimer's
by Richard Olsen, Ezra Ehrenkrantz, & Barbara Hutchings
1993 (77 pp.)
   NJIT Press
   New Jersey Institute of Technology
   Newark, NJ 07102
This excellent book has information gathered from 90 "seasoned" caregivers. It includes a wealth of information about how to create a comfortable and safe environment for a person with Alzheimer's.

Ideas for Making Your Home Accessible
by Betty Garee
1992 (94 pp.) $6.50
   Accent Special Publications
   Cheever Publishing, Inc.
   P.O. Box 700
   Bloomington, IL 61702
A small, practical book with many hints and illustrations related to accessibility in your home.

Lighthouse National Center for Vision and Aging (NCVA)
   800 Second Avenue
   New York, NY 10017
   (800) 334-5497
Information on vision problems faced by older people. Community education materials available for fee.

J.C.Penney
Easy Dressing Fashions Catalog: Favorites in No-Hassle Designs for Men and Women
   (800) 222-6161
Fashionable men's and women's clothing with Velcro fasteners, as well as selected, easy-to-wear items from the regular catalog.

Making Life More Livable: A Practical Guide to Over 1,000 Products and Resources for Living Well in the Mature Years
by Ellen Lederman
ISBN 0-671-87531-0
1994 (333 pp.)
   Simon & Schuster, New York
Provides information on products and services that can allow an older person to remain self-reliant and continue to pursue the activities that he or she enjoys—cooking, gardening, reading, television, traveling, and much, much more.

National Diabetes Information Clearinghouse (NDIC)
   Box NDIC
   Bethesda, MD 20892
   (301) 468-2162

National Stroke Association
   300 East Hampden Avenue, Suite 240
   Englewood, CO 80110
   (800) 787-6537
Information and education for individuals and families. Membership ($10.00) includes quarterly newsletter, "Be Stroke Smart."

Resources Conservation Company
> P.O. Box 71
> Greenwich, CT 06836
> (203) 964-0600

Resources for Elders with Disabilities
ISBN 0-929718-11-9
1993 (302 pp.) $43.95
> Resources for Rehabilitation
> 33 Bedford Street, Suite 19A
> Lexington, MA 02173

Large-print, excellent resource book. Includes extensive lists of resource organizations, publications, and services. Plentiful information about rehabilitation, laws that affect elders, and self-help groups. Chapters on specific disabilities and conditions with information about where to find specific services, adaptations, and publications.

Safety for Older Consumers: Home Safety Checklist
(29 pp.) Free.
> U.S. Consumer Product Safety
> Commission
> Washington, DC 20207
> (800) 638-2772

An excellent checklist and book with sensible safety precautions for older people.

Sears Health Care Products
> P.O. Box 7003
> Downers Grove, IL 60515
> (800) 326-1750

A complete catalog of specialty items readily available with Sears shopping convenience.

Self Help for the Hard of Hearing (SHHH)
> 7800 Wisconsin Avenue
> Bethesda, MD 20814
> (301) 657-2248

National organization that provides information, support, and referrals. Membership includes subscription to their magazine, *SHHH*.

Travel Information Center
> Moss Rehabilitation Hospital
> 12th and Tabor Road
> Philadelphia, PA 19141
> (215) 456-9600

Provides worldwide travel and accessibility information for a small fee.

Wheeling to Fire Safety: Fire Emergency Procedures for Individuals with Disabilities
Available from:
> Eastern Paralyzed Veterans Association
> 75-20 Astoria Boulevard
> Jackson Heights, NY 11370-1178
> (718) 803-EPVA

ABOUT THE AUTHOR

Doreen Brenner Greenstein is a developmental psychologist at Cornell University. Her background is in rehabilitation counseling, and one of her passions is low-tech assistive technology. Perhaps because she has lived on a farm for the past thirty years and has seen how much can be done using simple materials, her interest in assistive technology has grown to include homemade solutions and simple "fixing and tinkering" that can help people maintain their independence in the community. She wants everyone to know that the folks on the book cover are her parents, Michael and Paula Brenner.

ABOUT THE ILLUSTRATOR

Suzanne Bloom has created note cards for the New York State Citizens' Coalition for Children, contributed drawings to the Harcourt Brace Emergent Readers series, and written and illustrated two children's picture books: *We Keep a Pig in the Parlor* and the award-winning *A Family for Jamie.* A graduate of Cooper Union, Suzanne traded in city sidewalks for a 10-acre wooded backyard in rural New York. At home, with her husband and two sons, there's never a shortage of encouragement, critiques or inspiration. She balances the solitude of the studio with artist-visits to elementary schools.

Also Available from Brookline Books

BACKYARDS AND BUTTERFLIES:
Ways to Include Children with Disabilities
in Outdoor Activities

by Doreen Greenstein, Ph.D., Cornell University;
Naomi Miner, O.T.R./L.; & Emilie Kudela, M.Ed.

Illustrated by Suzanne Bloom, B.F.A.

Dozens of imaginative ideas for making outdoor activities accessible to children with physical disabilities. This book gives easy-to-follow "how-to" directions — accompanied by attractive and colorful illustrations — for constructing homemade assistive devices, using common household and hardware store materials. **Sections include:** Gardening • Nature • Caring for Animals • Wheels • Swings & Slides • Backyards • and more!

"Gives suggestions to make playing and exploring in the outdoors as easy for a child with disabilities as for their able-bodied family members, and is conscientious about providing safety information and recommendations."—**OT Week**, *American Occupational Therapy Association*

Title Code: BYAP
ISBN: 1-57129-011-7
Price: $14.95 softcover

To order, call 1-800-666-BOOK